SACRED OPERATING SYSTEM

Introduction	5
Chapter 1: Lex Primatus - The Law of Primacy	12
Chapter 2: Lex Transcendentiae - The Law of Transcendence	29
Chapter 3: Lex Integritatis - The Law of Integrity	47
Chapter 4: Lex Aequilibrii - The Law of Balance	65
Chapter 5: Lex Honoris - The Law of Honour	82
Chapter 6: Lex Vitae - The Law of Life	101
Chapter 7: Lex Fidelitatis - The Law of Fidelity	119
Chapter 8: Lex Proprietatis - The Law of Property	138
Chapter 9: Lex Veritatis - The Law of Truth	155
Chapter 10: Lex Contentamenti - The Law of Contentment	172
CHAPTER 11: Why These Laws Work (Even If You Don't Believe in God)	189
CHAPTER 12: What Happens When a Society Ignores Them	209
EPILOGUE: The Return of Ancient Wisdom	221
References	230

Foreword & Acknowledgements

Ever since learning about the idea of the 'Lindy Effect', it has been obvious to me that the Bible is a very clear example of it.

Nassim Nicholas Taleb popularised the concept in *Antifragile*, building on earlier formulations. The Lindy Effect states that for **non-perishable things**—ideas, books, technologies—their **future life expectancy is proportional to their current age**. So, if a concept has survived 100 years, it's statistically more likely to survive another 100.

The truths contained in the Bible, is at the very least the received wisdom of the ages. As such, it is very likely to have salience in modernity too, and I wanted to test this hypothesis.

Instead of focussing on all truths of the Bible (an impossible task) I chose the ten commandments to investigate the claim,

My research assistant, as is the way today, was a large language model – principally Manus AI. Whilst Manus did the heavy lifting of research and editing, the IDEAS and the message are mine. Manus was helpful in finding examples and even getting the facts straight. (I would have said Lex Veritas, not Lex Veritatis because my Latin is just not that good.)

I have the privilege to spend much of my time reading, researching and writing, since retiring from full-time work.

But this privilege is gifted to me by the grace of my wife, Moonyeen. She has the patience of a saint.

But we have lived our life; our children have much more to live, and it is for them that I wanted to gather these thoughts as well: Megan, Lauraine and Matthew.

And finally, YOU, dear reader for spending some of the time you have, along with some money, to explore these ideas with me.

God Bless You All.

Dennis Price
Kiama, Australia.

2 January 2026

Introduction

Why Ancient Rules Refuse to Die

There is a quiet assumption in modern culture that anything ancient must be naive, oppressive, or obsolete. We live in an age of neuroscience, psychology, and data; an age that prides itself on having outgrown superstition and moral absolutes. Against that backdrop, the Ten Commandments seem like relics — rigid rules issued by a distant, temperamental deity to a pre-scientific people who did not yet understand the world.

And yet, something odd keeps happening.

The more confidently modern society dismisses these laws, the more it appears to reproduce the very failures they were designed to prevent. Anxiety rises. Trust collapses. Families fragment. Meaning erodes. Institutions decay. Loneliness becomes endemic. Public discourse hardens into tribal hostility. Despite unprecedented comfort, people report feeling more lost, more exhausted, and more divided than ever.

This raises an uncomfortable question:

What if the problem is not that the commandments are outdated — but that they serve the purpose of empowering humans to live a full life?

What if they were, instead, early observations about human nature, distilled into moral language? What if these divine commands describe psychological realities? And what if ignoring them carries consequences - whether or not one believes in God?

This book explores that possibility.

The Mistake We Make About "Ancient Morality"

Modern readers often approach the Ten Commandments as a list of prohibitions issued by authority:

Do this. Don't do that. Obey or be punished.

But that framing misunderstands how ancient moral systems functioned.

The commandments are not written like legislation. They function more like boundaries for human behavior — guardrails rather than threats. They do not explain *why* the rules exist, only *that they do*. And that omission is revealing. The text assumes something we have largely forgotten:

> That certain patterns of behaviour reliably lead to human flourishing, and others reliably lead to destruction.

In other words, the commandments are equally divine orders that function as psychological axioms. They describe what happens when human beings violate fundamental constraints of their own nature. Some argue that these are gifts from a benevolent God; but if you don't believe that, the common grace of God (we believe) extends to all. So, irrespective of what the source is or is not, the benefits extend to all.

To make this book accessible to all, I lean on psychology and neuroscience to convey the benefits of God's law.

The Modern Blind Spot

Today, we tend to believe that morality is socially constructed — that values evolve as societies evolve, and that ancient norms can be discarded once they conflict with modern preferences.

Yet psychology tells a different story.

Across cultures and centuries, the same behavioral patterns produce the same outcomes:

- Betrayal destroys trust.
- Envy corrodes happiness.
- Lies collapse cooperation.
- Overwork leads to burnout.
- Sexual instability destabilizes families.
- Disregard for truth fractures societies.

These patterns do not depend on religion. They appear in secular cultures, in corporations, in relationships, and in political systems. They are observable, repeatable, and increasingly measurable.

Neuroscience, evolutionary psychology, and behavioral economics now describe — in clinical language — what the commandments expressed in moral form thousands of years ago.

The difference is not 'content'.

It is vocabulary.

The Commandments as Psychological Architecture

The central claim of this book is simple:

The Ten Commandments function as a compressed map of human psychological – and consequently

societal – stability.

They are not random.

They are not arbitrary.

They describe:

- How humans orient meaning
- How trust is formed and destroyed
- How desire destabilises perception
- How societies maintain cohesion
- How individuals avoid self-destruction

Each commandment targets a pressure point in human nature — a place where, if left unchecked, cognition, relationships, or communities begin to unravel.

Seen this way, the commandments extends to also being:

- a cognitive operating system,
- a social stability protocol,
- or a moral immune system.

They are not about obedience as much as they are about alignment that *follows* from obedience.

Why This Matters Now

We are living through an era of extraordinary contradiction.

We have more information than any generation in history — yet less consensus on what is true.

We have more freedom — yet more anxiety.

More connectivity — yet more loneliness.

More choice — yet less meaning.

We are told that fulfillment comes from self-expression, autonomy, and liberation from constraints. And yet, mental health statistics move in the opposite direction.

I argue that the problem is not freedom itself, but **freedom without structure**.

The commandments, stripped of religious language, describe the psychological structures that make freedom survivable. Ignore them, and life does not become freer — it becomes unstable.

This approach may make them more palatable, so to speak. My aim is not to proselytize or convert the casual reader, but to raise awareness of the intrinsic value of God's sacred operating system. (Thinking and living with that operation system will do the job of drawing you closer to God in due course.)

What This Book Is — and Is Not

This is not a (direct) religious defense of Christianity.

It is not an argument for blind faith.

It is not a political manifesto.

It is an examination of:

- human behaviour,
- cognitive limits,
- social trust,
- and the unintended consequences of moral abandonment.

You do not need to believe in God to understand the argument–even if I hope you do.

But you may find yourself reconsidering why these ideas survived for thousands of years while countless others vanished.

The Path Forward

Each chapter will take one commandment and do three things:

1. **Explain its original meaning**

   Free from dogma, grounded in historical and psychological context.

2. **Translate it into modern cognitive terms**

   Using neuroscience, behavioural science, and sociology.

3. **Show what happens when it is ignored**

In individuals, institutions, and entire cultures.

By the end, the question will no longer be:

"Do these rules still apply?"

But rather:

"Can we afford to keep pretending they don't?"

And then, possibly explore who the benevolent God is that set those boundaries for human flourishing.

Chapter 1: Lex Primatus - The Law of Primacy

> *You shall have no other gods before me. (Exodus 20:3)*

In the late 1990s, a peculiar cultural phenomenon began to take shape in the sprawling suburbs of America, a quiet revolution not of politics or protest, but of plastic. It was the era of the Beanie Baby, a collection of floppy, under-stuffed plush toys that, for a brief, bewildering period, became one of the most sought-after commodities on the planet. At its peak, the manufacturer, Ty Inc., was reportedly earning over $700 million in a single year. Ordinary people, from stay-at-home mothers to seasoned investors, were caught in a speculative frenzy, convinced that these pellet-filled animals were not just toys, but a new class of appreciating asset. Stories abounded of people pouring their life savings into collections, of families driving across state lines on the rumour of a rare find, and of a secondary market where a $5 toy could fetch thousands.

One particularly poignant story from that time is of a family who, believing they were securing their children's future, invested over $100,000 in thousands of Beanie Babies, storing them meticulously in airtight containers. They weren't just collecting; they were worshipping at the altar of a false financial god. The toy animals had ceased to be objects of play and had become the central organising principle of their economic lives, their ultimate concern. When the bubble inevitably burst in 1999, leaving the market saturated and the once-rare items virtually worthless, the family was financially and emotionally devastated. Their story, and countless others like it, is a vivid, if somewhat absurd, illustration of a principle so fundamental to human psychology that it was codified as the very first of the Ten Commandments: the Law of Primacy.

"You shall have no other gods before me."

Stripped of its ancient, theological language, this command makes a profound psychological claim: human beings are constitutionally incapable of not having a "god." We are, by nature, worshipping creatures. Something will always occupy the highest place in our cognitive and motivational hierarchy. This is not a threat, but a statement of fact about our operating system. That supreme value—be it financial security, political ideology, social status, romantic love, or even the self—functions as our god. It is the orienting principle around which our perceptions, thoughts, and actions are organised. It is the ultimate arbiter of our decisions, the source from which we derive our sense of meaning, purpose, and identity. The First Commandment is not merely a religious injunction for the pious; it is a user manual for the human mind. It argues that the *quality* of our ultimate concern is the single most important determinant of our individual and collective well-being. When that highest value is unstable, false, or too small to carry the weight of our worship, everything beneath it fractures.

The Unavoidable Hierarchy

To function in the world, we must simplify it. The sheer volume of information bombarding our senses at any given moment is overwhelming. As you read this sentence, your brain is filtering out the sensation of the chair beneath you, the ambient noise in the room, the feeling of your clothes on your skin, and a million other potential distractions. This filtering process isn't random; it's directed by your goals.

Your brain prioritises what is relevant to your current aim—in this case, understanding this text—and relegates everything else to the background. This is the essence of what psychologists call a **value hierarchy**. It's the cognitive structure that allows us to navigate complexity without being paralysed by it.

At the very top of this structure sits our ultimate concern, our "god." This dominant value acts like a cognitive North Star, orienting our entire perceptual framework. If your highest value is professional success, you will perceive the world primarily in terms of opportunities and threats to your career. A networking event becomes a field of opportunity; a critical comment from a colleague becomes a significant threat. If your highest value is the well-being of your children, you will interpret the world through a lens of safety and danger to them. A news report about a local crime is not just information; it is a direct, personal warning. This is not a conscious choice; it is an automatic, pre-rational process. Our highest value dictates what we see.

Modern neuroscience provides a compelling picture of how this works. The brain's **dopamine system**, often misunderstood as a simple "pleasure chemical," is more accurately described as the engine of motivation and goal pursuit. As researchers Ethan Bromberg-Martin, Masayuki Matsumoto, and Okihide Hikosaka explained in a landmark 2010 paper in *Neuron*, dopamine is not just about reward; it's about motivational salience. It drives us towards what our brain has tagged as important. When a particular goal is elevated to the status of a god, the dopamine system goes into overdrive, fixating our attention and driving our behaviour relentlessly towards that end. All other potential goals and values are downregulated, their motivational power diminished. We become, in a very real sense, neurologically blind to anything that does not serve our chosen deity.

This neurological reality has profound practical implications. Consider the phenomenon of **decision fatigue**, a well-documented psychological effect where the quality of our decisions deteriorates after making many choices in succession. When we are cognitively depleted, we default to our highest values. A person whose god is convenience will choose fast food over a healthy meal. A person whose god is social approval will make choices that please others rather than serve their own genuine needs. A person whose god is the avoidance of conflict will capitulate rather than stand firm on principle. Our ultimate concern is the gravitational centre of our decision-making, especially when our cognitive resources are low.

This is the psychological genius of the First Commandment. It recognises that because we *must* have a value hierarchy, the most important question is not *whether* we worship, but *what* we worship. The command to place God at the apex of this hierarchy is a prescription for psychological stability. It proposes that orienting our lives around an ultimate value that is transcendent, infinite, and good provides the most robust and resilient framework for human flourishing. When we attempt to place something finite and created—money, power, a nation, a political ideology, another person, or even ourselves—in that ultimate position, we are setting ourselves up for an inevitable collapse. These lesser gods are too small for the throne of the human heart, and when they fail, the entire structure of our meaning comes crashing down.

The Gods of the Modern Age

If the idea of worshipping false gods seems like a relic of a bygone era, a concern for people who bowed down to golden calves, we need only look at the pathologies of our own time. We may not erect stone idols, but our modern pantheon is just as real and, arguably, far more insidious. We have simply substituted the old gods of wood and stone for new gods of ideology, consumerism, and the self.

The God of the Marketplace: Consumerism

Consider the case of the Beanie Baby craze. It was a classic example of what happens when the pursuit of material wealth becomes an ultimate concern. The logic of the market—acquisition, speculation, and profit—became the organising principle for thousands of people's lives. Their days were consumed by the hunt, their conversations dominated by rarity and resale value, their hopes pinned on the ever-inflating bubble. This is consumerism as a god. It promises fulfilment through acquisition, identity through brands, and security through wealth. But it is a fickle and demanding deity.

The psychological cost of this worship is what many now call **consumer burnout**. It is a state of chronic exhaustion, cynicism, and a pervasive sense of emptiness that arises from the relentless pressure to acquire and compare. The **hedonic treadmill**, a concept well-established in psychology, describes our tendency to quickly return to a relatively stable level of happiness despite major positive or negative life events. A new car, a bigger house, the latest smartphone—they all provide a temporary jolt of satisfaction, a dopamine hit that quickly fades, leaving us needing the next, bigger, better thing to feel the same rush. This endless cycle of desire and disappointment is the liturgy of the consumer god, and it leads not to lasting happiness, but to anxiety, debt, and a profound sense of meaninglessness.

Research by psychologists Ed Diener and colleagues has shown that whilst people do experience temporary increases in happiness after positive events like winning the lottery or getting a promotion, they typically return to their baseline level of well-being within a relatively short period. The problem is not that material goods provide no pleasure—they do—but that they cannot provide *lasting* meaning. When consumerism becomes our god, we are chasing a satisfaction that is, by its very nature, fleeting. We work jobs we dislike to buy things we don't need to impress people we don't like. It is a hollow pursuit, a spiritual dead end.

The tragedy is that many people only realise this after decades of faithful service to the consumer god. They reach the pinnacle of material success only to discover that the view from the top is not what they expected. The house is bigger, but it feels emptier. The wardrobe is fuller, but the soul is more impoverished. This is the inevitable outcome when we place a finite good—material wealth—in the position of an infinite concern.

The God of the Tribe: Political Ideology

Perhaps no modern god is more voracious than that of political ideology. In an age of declining religious affiliation and fragmenting communities, many people have turned to politics to find the sense of identity, belonging, and moral certainty that were once provided by faith. Political tribes offer a clear-cut world of heroes and villains, of in-groups and out-groups. They provide a shared narrative, a common enemy, and a sense of righteous purpose. The psychological mechanism at play here is what researchers call **identity fusion**, a visceral feeling of oneness with a group where the boundaries between the self and the collective blur.

As the evolutionary psychologist Robert Lynch has noted, this fusion can be a powerful force for cooperation, but it has a profoundly dark side. When a political ideology becomes our ultimate concern, it triggers our most primitive tribal instincts. Our capacity for reason is hijacked by our need to belong. We engage in motivated reasoning, uncritically accepting information that confirms our tribe's narrative and aggressively rejecting anything that challenges it. Studies by psychologist Leor Zmigrod at the University of Cambridge have found that cognitive inflexibility—the inability to adapt one's thinking in response to new information—is a strong predictor of extremist attitudes, including a willingness to endorse violence against out-groups.

This is the path to **dehumanisation**. Opponents are no longer people with different opinions; they are malevolent, sub-human enemies who must be defeated, silenced, or eliminated. The Rwandan genocide, where Hutu extremists used radio broadcasts to label their Tutsi neighbours as "cockroaches" before slaughtering them by the hundreds of thousands, is a horrifying testament to where this path leads. The language of dehumanisation—"vermin," "animals," "parasites"—has a dark and consistent history. It precedes atrocity. It is the linguistic preparation for violence.

Whilst our current political climate may seem far removed from such atrocities, the underlying psychological process is the same. When we elevate a political tribe to the status of a god, we are playing with the fire of our most dangerous evolutionary inheritance. Online discourse is increasingly characterised by this dehumanising language. Comment sections are rife with explicit descriptions of political opponents as "sub-human" or "non-human." The ease with which we can dismiss the humanity of those who disagree with us is a warning sign. It suggests that for many, political ideology has become not just a set of policy preferences, but an ultimate concern, a god that demands absolute loyalty and justifies any means.

The antidote to this pathology is not political disengagement, but a proper ordering of values. When our ultimate concern is something higher than our tribe—a commitment to truth, to human dignity, to the imago Dei in every person—we can participate in politics without being consumed by it. We can advocate for our beliefs without demonising those who disagree. We can be passionate without being possessed.

The God of the Self: Narcissism

Finally, we come to the most seductive and perhaps most destructive idol of our time: the self. In a culture that champions radical individualism, self-expression, and personal autonomy as the highest goods, it is little wonder that many of us have made ourselves the centre of our own universe. The self-as-god promises ultimate freedom and control. It whispers that our feelings are the ultimate authority, that our desires are self-justifying, and that our personal happiness is the most important goal in life.

The rise of social media has poured fuel on this fire, creating a global stage for the performance of the self. We curate idealised versions of our lives, chasing likes and followers as validation of our worth. This has contributed to what many psychologists have termed a **narcissism epidemic**. Narcissism, in this context, is not just vanity; it is a psychological state characterised by an inflated sense of self-importance, a deep need for excessive attention and admiration, troubled relationships, and a lack of empathy for others. Research by psychologists Jean Twenge and W. Keith Campbell has documented a significant rise in narcissistic traits amongst young people over recent decades, correlating with the rise of social media and a cultural emphasis on self-esteem above all else.

The individual who worships at the altar of self becomes fragile, hypersensitive to criticism, and incapable of the kind of self-transcendence that Viktor Frankl, the Austrian psychiatrist and Holocaust survivor, identified as the true source of human meaning. Frankl's story is one of the most powerful refutations of the self-as-god that we possess. Between 1942 and 1945, Frankl was imprisoned in four Nazi concentration camps, including Auschwitz. He endured unimaginable suffering, lost his wife, parents, and brother, and witnessed daily atrocities that would break most people. Yet he not only survived, but emerged with a profound insight into the nature of human resilience.

In his seminal book *Man's Search for Meaning*, Frankl argued powerfully against the idea that self-actualisation is the ultimate goal. Based on his experiences in the camps, he observed that the people most likely to survive were not those who were physically strongest, nor those who were most focused on their own survival or happiness. Rather, they were those who had a purpose outside of themselves—a loved one to return to, a work to complete, a meaning to fulfil. Frankl wrote, "It is a peculiarity of man that he can only live by looking to the future… And this is his salvation in the most difficult moments of his existence, although he sometimes has to force his mind to the task."

Frankl described one particularly harrowing moment when he was forced to march through the frozen countryside, his feet covered in open wounds, his body emaciated from starvation. In that moment of extreme suffering, he began to think of his wife, not knowing she had already been killed in another camp. He imagined her face, her smile, her presence. He realised, in that instant, that love transcends the physical presence of the beloved. The meaning he derived from that love, from that connection to something beyond himself, gave him the strength to take the next step, and the next, and the next. This is the power of self-transcendence. This is what happens when our ultimate concern is not the self, but something infinitely greater.

When the self is the highest value, life becomes a closed loop. We become trapped in the echo chamber of our own needs and desires, and the inevitable sufferings of life become not opportunities for growth, but intolerable personal insults. The god of self is a cruel master, promising everything and delivering only a fragile, anxious, and ultimately empty existence. As Frankl observed, "Mental health is based on a certain degree of tension, the tension between what one has already achieved and what one still ought to accomplish, or the gap between what one is and what one should become." When the self is god, there is no "ought," no "should," no call from beyond the self. There is only the tyranny of our own desires, which are never satisfied.

The Architecture of Order

The First Commandment, then, is not an arbitrary rule. It is a profound insight into the architecture of human cognition and the necessary conditions for psychological and social stability. It makes the radical claim that our lives are ordered, or disordered, from the top down. The nature of our ultimate commitment—our 'god'—determines the stability of everything else. If our god is money, we will be subject to the boom and bust of the market. If our god is a political tribe, we will be swept away by the tides of polarisation and hatred. If our god is the self, we will be crushed by the burden of our own finitude and fragility.

Choose your 'God' wisely because it will ruin or rule your life.

The command to have no other gods is an invitation to build our lives on a foundation that is truly ultimate, truly transcendent, and truly good. It is a call to orient ourselves around a reality that is not subject to the whims of the market, the passions of the tribe, or the insecurities of the ego. For the ancient Israelites, and for Christians today, that reality is the God revealed in scripture—a God of love, justice, and mercy, who created humanity for a purpose that transcends the self. This God is not a projection of human desires, but the source of all being, the ground of all value, the ultimate reality to which all lesser realities point.

But even for those who do not share this faith, the psychological principle holds true. As the late author David Foster Wallace put it in his famous commencement speech, "There is no such thing as not worshipping. Everybody worships. The only choice we get is what to worship. And the compelling reason for maybe choosing some sort of god or spiritual-type thing to worship… is that pretty much anything else you worship will eat you alive."

Wallace went on to describe the consequences of worshipping the wrong gods with brutal honesty: "If you worship money and things, if they are where you tap real meaning in life, then you will never have enough, never feel you have enough. It's the truth. Worship your body and beauty and sexual allure and you will always feel ugly. And when time and age start showing, you will die a million deaths before they finally grieve you... Worship power, you will end up feeling weak and afraid, and you will need ever more power over others to numb you to your own fear. Worship your intellect, being seen as smart, you will end up feeling stupid, a fraud, always on the verge of being found out."

This is not religious moralising; it is psychological observation. The gods we choose shape the lives we live. They determine what we see, what we value, what we pursue, and ultimately, who we become. The Law of Primacy forces us to confront the most important question of our lives: What sits on the throne of our hearts? What is our ultimate concern?

For whatever we place there, that will be our god. And that god will shape everything. The quality of our relationships, the resilience of our mental health, the depth of our joy, the meaning we find in suffering, the legacy we leave behind—all of it flows from this single, foundational choice. When the highest value is unstable or false, everything beneath it fractures. But when the highest value is truly ultimate, truly good, truly transcendent, it provides an unshakeable foundation for a life of genuine flourishing.

This is why the First Commandment comes first. It is not just chronologically first in the list; it is logically first in the architecture of human well-being. Get this right, and everything else has a chance to fall into place. Get this wrong, and no amount of effort in other areas can compensate for the fundamental instability at the core. The Law of Primacy is not a restriction; it is a liberation. It frees us from the tyranny of false gods and invites us into the stability of true worship.

The Practical Test

How, then, do we identify our true god? How do we know what sits at the apex of our value hierarchy? The answer is simpler than we might think, though often uncomfortable to confront. Our god is revealed not by what we say we value, but by what we actually do. It is revealed in how we spend our time, our money, and our mental energy. It is revealed in what makes us anxious, what makes us angry, and what we cannot imagine living without.

Consider your own life for a moment. What is the first thing you think about when you wake up in the morning? What occupies your mind during idle moments? What would devastate you if you lost it? What do you sacrifice other goods to obtain or maintain? These questions are diagnostic. They reveal the functional god of your life, which may be quite different from the god you profess to worship.

A person may claim that family is their highest value, but if they consistently sacrifice time with their children for career advancement, their functional god is professional success. A person may claim to value health, but if they consistently choose immediate gratification over long-term well-being, their functional god is pleasure. A person may claim to value truth, but if they consistently consume only media that confirms their existing beliefs, their functional god is ideological certainty. The gap between our professed values and our revealed values is often vast, and it is in this gap that much of our psychological suffering resides.

This is not to suggest that career, pleasure, or certainty are bad things. They are not. They are good things. The problem arises when good things are made into ultimate things. When a 'good thing' becomes a 'god thing', it becomes a 'bad thing'. It demands a level of devotion and provides a level of meaning that it was never designed to carry. The result is inevitable disappointment, anxiety, and a sense of existential fragility.

The Christian answer to this dilemma is not to eliminate these lesser goods, but to properly order them beneath an ultimate good that is truly capable of bearing the weight of our worship. When God—the infinite, eternal, all-good Creator—is placed at the apex of our value hierarchy, all other goods find their proper place. Career becomes a calling, a means of serving others and stewarding our gifts, rather than a source of identity. Pleasure becomes a gift to be enjoyed with gratitude, rather than a god to be pursued at all costs. Relationships become opportunities for love and service, rather than vehicles for our own validation. Even suffering can be integrated into a meaningful narrative when it is understood within the context of a larger purpose. (Arguably, it may be the *only* way to integrate suffering–a natural condition of the world– properly and effectively.)

This is not merely theoretical. It has been tested in the most extreme circumstances imaginable. Frankl's observations in the concentration camps were not abstract philosophical musings; they were empirical observations of what actually sustained human beings in the face of unimaginable horror. Those who had an ultimate concern that transcended their immediate circumstances—a God to pray to, a loved one to return to, a work to complete—were more likely to survive. Those whose ultimate concern was their own comfort, their own survival, their own self, were more likely to succumb to despair.

One of Frankl's most powerful examples was of a fellow prisoner who had a dream that the war would end on a specific date. As that date approached, the man's hope grew. But when the date came and went, and the war continued, the man's hope collapsed. He fell ill and died shortly thereafter. Frankl observed that it was not the physical conditions that killed him—many others survived in the same conditions—but the loss of his future, the collapse of his meaning. His hope had been placed in a finite thing—a specific date—rather than in something transcendent. When that finite hope failed, he had nothing left to sustain him.

Contrast this with Frankl's own experience. His hope was not pinned to a specific date or outcome, but to a larger sense of meaning and purpose. Even in the midst of suffering, he was able to find moments of profound beauty and significance. He described one evening when, after a brutal day of forced labour, the prisoners were marched back to camp. The sunset was spectacular, and despite their exhaustion and pain, the prisoners stopped to admire it. Someone remarked on its beauty, and for a moment, they were not prisoners, not victims, but human beings capable of appreciating beauty, of transcending their circumstances. This is the power of a properly ordered value hierarchy. It allows us to find meaning even in suffering, beauty even in darkness, hope even in despair.

The Path Forward

The Law of Primacy, then, is both a diagnosis and a prescription. It diagnoses the fundamental problem of human existence: we are worshipping creatures who will inevitably place something at the centre of our lives, and the quality of that central commitment determines the quality of everything else. It prescribes the solution: place at the centre something that is truly ultimate, truly transcendent, truly good.

For the Christian, this means placing the God of the Bible at the apex of the value hierarchy. It means recognising that we were created by a good God, for a good purpose, and that our deepest fulfilment comes not from serving ourselves, but from serving Him and, through Him, serving others. It means understanding that the commandment to have no other gods is not a restriction on our freedom, but a revelation of the conditions necessary for genuine freedom. We are most free when we are rightly ordered, when our loves are properly arranged, when our worship is directed towards that which is truly worthy of worship.

But even for those who do not share this faith, the psychological principle remains valid. The question is not whether you will worship, but what you will worship. Choose carefully. Your god will shape your life. It will determine what you see, what you value, what you pursue, and who you become. Choose a god that is too small, and you will live a small life, characterised by anxiety, fragility, and eventual collapse. Choose a god that is truly ultimate, and you will have a foundation that can withstand the storms of life, a source of meaning that cannot be taken from you, and a hope that endures even in the darkest night.

The First Commandment is not the beginning of a list of arbitrary rules. It is the foundation of a comprehensive vision of human flourishing. It is the recognition that we are not self-sufficient, self-creating, self-sustaining beings. We are creatures who need something beyond ourselves to orient our lives, to give us meaning, to call us towards something greater than our own immediate desires. When we acknowledge this need and direct our worship towards that which is truly worthy, we discover not restriction, but liberation. Not burden, but rest. Not slavery, but freedom.

This is the Law of Primacy. And it is the beginning of wisdom.

Chapter 2: Lex Transcendentiae - The Law of Transcendence

You shall not make for yourself a graven image, or any likeness of anything that is in heaven above, or that is in the earth beneath, or that is in the water under the earth. (Exodus 20:4)

In September 2024, a couple in their sixties, vacationing in the idyllic coastal town of Isle of Palms, South Carolina, found themselves in a situation that was anything but serene. Following the calm, authoritative voice of their GPS, they made a turn, expecting a road but finding only the dark, churning water of a marina. Their SUV plunged off the boat ramp, and in an instant, their holiday became a fight for survival. By a stroke of sheer luck, their windows were down, preventing the immense water pressure from sealing them in a metallic tomb. A bartender from a nearby restaurant, a former lifeguard, saw the splash and reacted instantly, diving in and pulling the disoriented couple from their sinking vehicle. They survived, shaken but unharmed, joining a growing and rather bewildered club of people who have been led into peril by their satellite navigation systems. The phenomenon has become so common that it has earned its own grim moniker: "Death by GPS."

These incidents, which range from the comical to the tragic, are a perfect, if terrifying, metaphor for a fundamental error in human cognition. A driver, eyes glued to the small, glowing screen, places more trust in the digital representation of the world than in the world itself. The GPS says, "Turn here," and so they turn, even when their own eyes can plainly see that "here" is a lake, a cliff, or a set of railway tracks. They have committed a cardinal error, one so basic it was immortalised thousands of years ago as the Second Commandment. They have confused the map for the territory. And in doing so, they have begun to worship a false god.

"You shall not make for yourself a graven image."

This command, coming directly after the injunction to have no other gods, is not merely a prohibition against carving idols out of wood or stone. It is a profound psychological warning against the dangers of reductionism. It is a command against worshipping our own simplified models of reality. A graven image is a map—a finite, human-made, simplified representation of a reality that is infinitely more complex. The First Commandment tells us *what* to worship; the Second tells us *how*. It insists that the object of our ultimate concern must be transcendent, meaning it cannot be fully captured, contained, or controlled by any of our mental models. The moment we fall in love with our map, the moment we mistake our simplified model for the thing itself, we have created a graven image. And the moment we worship it, we stop learning, we stop growing, and we become dangerously detached from the truth.

The Map Is Not the Territory

In 1931, the Polish-American philosopher and engineer Alfred Korzybski, in a paper on mathematical semantics, coined a phrase that would echo through the fields of psychology, philosophy, and computer science: "The map is not the territory." It's a simple, powerful idea. We navigate the world not by engaging with its full, overwhelming complexity, but by creating and using mental models, or "maps." These maps are essential. Without them, we would be paralysed, unable to make decisions or function at all. A scientific theory is a map. A political ideology is a map. A company's business plan is a map. Even our perception of a friend or a spouse is a map, a simplified model of an infinitely complex person.

The problem arises when we forget that we are dealing with a map. We start to treat our simplified representation as if it were the complete, unvarnished reality. This is not just a philosophical error; it is a deeply ingrained cognitive bias. Our brains are wired to seek certainty and to conserve energy. It is far easier to operate from a fixed, simple model than to constantly update our understanding based on new, often contradictory, information from the messy, complex territory of the real world.

This drive for certainty is what psychologists, led by Arie Kruglanski, call the **need for cognitive closure**. It is a desire for a clear, firm answer to a question, an end to ambiguity. When this need is high, we tend to "seize and freeze" on the first piece of information that provides a sense of closure. We grab a map, any map, and we hold on tight. Once we have "frozen" on a belief, we become resistant to new information. We engage in motivated reasoning, seeking out evidence that confirms our map and dismissing evidence that challenges it. The map becomes a fortress, a defence against the anxiety of uncertainty. But in our quest for certainty, we sacrifice truth. We become cognitively rigid, unable to adapt when the territory inevitably changes or when we discover our map was flawed from the beginning.

This isn't just a modern psychological concept; it's a pattern visible throughout history. Consider the disastrous French invasion of Russia in 1812. Napoleon Bonaparte, one of the most brilliant military strategists in history, operated from a map of warfare that had been spectacularly successful across Europe. His model was based on rapid, decisive battles, living off the land, and forcing the enemy to the negotiating table after a swift defeat. This map was his graven image. When he invaded Russia, the territory refused to conform to his map. The Russians retreated, burning the land as they went, refusing to engage in the decisive battle Napoleon sought. His map told him that capturing Moscow would mean victory, but when he entered the city, he found it deserted and burning. His model of war was useless in the vast, unforgiving territory of the Russian winter. By clinging to his outdated map, by worshipping his own past successes, Napoleon led the Grande Armée to one of the most catastrophic military defeats in history. He mistook his map for the territory, and over half a million of his men paid the price.

A more recent, and equally devastating, example can be found in the lead-up to the 2008 Global Financial Crisis. The world's largest banks and investment firms had built sophisticated mathematical models—maps—to price and trade complex financial instruments like mortgage-backed securities and collateralised debt obligations. These models, often based on the Gaussian copula function, made a series of simplifying assumptions about how financial markets behaved. Crucially, they assumed that the risk of many thousands of individual mortgages all defaulting at once was vanishingly small. The map was elegant, mathematically beautiful, and, for a time, spectacularly profitable. Bankers and ratings agencies worshipped at its altar, convinced they had tamed risk. But the territory—the real-world American housing market, with its subprime loans and interconnected web of debt—was far messier and more fragile than the map suggested. When house prices began to fall, the impossible happened. Defaults cascaded through the system in a way the models had deemed impossible. The map was not the territory. The graven image of a risk-free financial system shattered, and the global economy was plunged into its worst crisis since the Great Depression. The architects of the system had fallen in love with their model, and the world paid the price.

The Second Commandment is a direct assault on this tendency. It commands us to orient our lives around a reality—God—that is, by definition, transcendent and therefore un-mappable. You cannot create a complete and accurate model of an infinite being. Any attempt to do so, any graven image, is an act of profound reductionism. It is an attempt to shrink the divine to the size of human comprehension, to tame the transcendent and make it manageable. Worshipping a graven image is, in essence, worshipping our own understanding. It is the ultimate act of cognitive closure, a declaration that our map is so good, we no longer need the territory. And this is the gateway to delusion.

The Modern Pantheon of Graven Images

We may no longer bow down to statues of Baal or Zeus, but our world is filled with modern graven images, sophisticated maps that we mistake for the territory and worship as gods. These idols are not made of wood or stone, but of data, ideology, and pixels. They are all the more dangerous for their subtlety.

The Idol of Scientism: Worshipping the Method

Science is arguably the most powerful map-making tool humanity has ever invented. The scientific method—a process of observation, hypothesis, experimentation, and verification—has allowed us to create astonishingly accurate and useful models of the physical world. It has cured diseases, split the atom, and sent probes to the outer reaches of our solar system. But a dangerous confusion has arisen between science as a method and **scientism** as an ideology.

As the physicist and writer Adam Frank explains, science is a method for asking questions about the natural world. Scientism, on the other hand, is the philosophical belief that science is the *only* path to objective truth. It is the belief that the scientific map *is* the territory. Scientism asserts that any phenomenon that cannot be measured, quantified, and explained by the scientific method—such as consciousness, morality, beauty, love, or purpose—is either an illusion or will eventually be reduced to a purely physical explanation. It is, as Wikipedia puts it, an "excessive belief in the power of scientific knowledge and techniques."

This is a graven image. It takes the powerful tool of science and turns it into an all-encompassing worldview, a reductionist idol that dismisses vast swathes of human experience. The scientist who says, "Love is just a chemical reaction in the brain," is no longer speaking as a scientist; they are speaking as a priest of scientism. They have mistaken their partial map (the neurochemistry of attraction) for the entire territory (the lived experience of love). This is not to devalue the map—understanding the neurochemistry is fascinating and useful—but to worship it as the whole truth is an act of profound intellectual hubris. It represents a failure of transcendence, a refusal to acknowledge that reality might be richer and more complex than our current scientific models can describe.

Consider the debate around free will. From a strictly reductionist, materialist perspective—the perspective of scientism—free will is an illusion. All our choices are simply the predetermined outcomes of a chain of physical causes, of neurons firing in the brain. The map of physics has no room for genuine agency. But this conclusion is a product of the map, not necessarily the territory. It is what happens when you assume that the only real things are the things your scientific instruments can measure. It dismisses the universal human experience of making choices, of feeling responsible for our actions, of deliberating between right and wrong. A true scientist acknowledges the limits of their map. They might say, "Within our current model of physics, we cannot account for free will." The priest of scientism says, "Free will does not exist." The first is an act of intellectual humility; the second is an act of idolatry. The Second Commandment warns against this, reminding us that any attempt to create a final, complete image of reality is doomed to fail, because reality itself points to a transcendent Creator who cannot be contained within our systems of thought.

The Idol of the Persona: Worshipping the Image

In the digital age, we have become masters at creating and curating images of ourselves. Social media profiles are not reflections of who we are; they are carefully constructed maps of who we want to be. We post our holiday photos but not our arguments, our career successes but not our failures, our perfect meals but not our lonely nights. We do the same with celebrities. We consume their public personas—their interviews, their Instagram feeds, their movie roles—and mistake this curated image for the actual person.

This can lead to what psychologists call **celebrity worship syndrome**, an obsessive fascination with the life of a public figure. It is the development of a **parasocial relationship**, a one-sided bond where the worshipper feels they know the celebrity as a friend, even though no real relationship exists. They have fallen in love not with a person, but with a graven image, a carefully manufactured map of a person.

Research by psychologists like Randy and Lori Sansone has shown that at its extreme, this form of worship is correlated with a host of psychological problems: cognitive rigidity, identity diffusion, dissociation, and poor mental health. The worshipper becomes so absorbed in the simplified, idealised map of the celebrity's life that their own, more complex and messy life, feels inadequate. They are worshipping a graven image, and it is, as David Foster Wallace warned, eating them alive.

Think of the tragic case of Ricardo López, the stalker of the Icelandic singer Björk. Over a period of months in 1996, López became completely absorbed in a parasocial relationship with her. He documented his obsession in an 800-page diary, detailing his fantasies, his feelings of inadequacy, and his growing rage when he learned she was in a relationship with another musician. His map of Björk—a pure, idealised being who existed only for him—was violently contradicted by the territory of her real life. Unable to cope with this discrepancy, he mailed a letter bomb rigged with acid to her home and then, on camera, killed himself. It is a horrifying, extreme example, but it illustrates the endpoint of worshipping the image. When the map becomes more real than the territory, and the territory fails to conform to the map, the result can be psychosis and violence. The Second Commandment's prohibition is a call to engage with the messy, complex, and often difficult territory of real human relationships, rather than retreating into the safe, simple, and ultimately empty worship of a two-dimensional image.

The Idol of the Echo Chamber: Worshipping the Algorithm

Perhaps the most insidious form of modern idolatry is one we participate in every time we go online. The algorithms that power our social media feeds and search results are designed to do one thing: give us more of what we already like. They learn our preferences and create a personalised map of the world, a **filter bubble** (a term coined by internet activist Eli Pariser) that shows us a reality it thinks we want to see. If we are politically conservative, our feed will be filled with conservative news and opinions. If we are passionate about a particular social cause, we will see a constant stream of content that confirms the righteousness of that cause.

We end up in an **echo chamber**, a closed-loop system where our existing beliefs are endlessly reinforced and dissenting views are nowhere to be found. Our map of the world becomes more and more detailed, but it also becomes more and more detached from the actual, diverse, and often contradictory territory of reality. We become increasingly certain of our own rightness, not because we have engaged with opposing views and found them wanting, but because we have never encountered them at all.

This is the digital equivalent of carving a graven image. We take our preferred model of the world, and the algorithm helps us build a shrine to it, decorating it with confirming data points and protecting it from the blasphemy of disagreement. We end up worshipping a model of reality that is, in large part, a reflection of our own biases. This leads to the extreme polarisation and cognitive rigidity we see in our society today. People on opposite sides of a political issue are no longer just disagreeing; they are living in different realities, looking at entirely different maps. The Second Commandment warns against this very thing. It insists that we must not worship our own creations, our own models of the world. We must remain open to a transcendent truth that exists outside of our personalised filter bubbles.

Consider the rise of the Flat Earth movement. In an age of satellite imagery and global air travel, the belief that the Earth is a flat disc should be a fringe, easily debunked idea. Instead, it has grown into a global community, fuelled almost entirely by YouTube algorithms. A person watches one Flat Earth video, and the recommendation engine suggests another, and another. Soon, their entire feed is a self-contained ecosystem of pseudo-scientific "proofs," conspiracy theories, and social reinforcement. They are not engaging with the territory of scientific evidence; they are living entirely within a map created by an algorithm designed to maximise engagement. They are worshipping a graven image of the cosmos, and in doing so, they have sealed themselves off from reality.

The Freedom of Transcendence

The Law of Transcendence, like the Law of Primacy before it, is not a restriction but a liberation. It frees us from the prison of our own minds, from the tyranny of our own limited models. By commanding us to worship a God who is inherently transcendent and un-mappable, it forces us into a state of intellectual humility. It reminds us that our understanding is always incomplete, that our best maps are still just maps, and that reality is always richer, deeper, and more mysterious than we can possibly imagine.

This is the foundation of all true learning and all true wisdom. The person who believes their map is the territory has stopped learning. They have achieved cognitive closure, and in doing so, they have sealed themselves off from the truth. The person who understands that their map is just a map, on the other hand, is always learning, always exploring, always updating their understanding. They can hold their beliefs strongly, but they hold them with the humility of knowing they might be wrong. They can use their models to navigate the world, but they are always paying attention to the territory, ready to correct their course when the map and the reality diverge.

This is the psychological genius of the Second Commandment. It is a built-in error-correction mechanism for the human mind. It prevents us from falling into the trap of reductionism, from worshipping our own intellectual creations. It calls us to a life of perpetual openness, of wonder, of a humble and relentless search for a truth that is always beyond our complete grasp. It is a call to worship the Creator, not the creation; the artist, not the painting; the territory, not the map. In a world of GPS-induced accidents, ideological echo chambers, and digital mirages, it is a command that is more relevant and more necessary than ever.

To worship a transcendent God is to acknowledge that there is a reality that exists independently of our perceptions, our models, and our desires. It is to accept that we are not the ultimate arbiters of truth. This is a profoundly liberating realisation. It frees us from the impossible burden of having to be right all the time. It allows us to be wrong, to make mistakes, to change our minds. It allows for grace, for forgiveness, for the possibility of redemption. A world without transcendence is a world without grace, because in such a world, there is no higher court of appeal, no standard of truth beyond our own fallible judgments. If my map is the territory, and your map is different, then one of us must be destroyed. But if we both acknowledge that our maps are imperfect representations of a higher, transcendent territory, then we can have dialogue. We can learn from each other. We can, together, create a better map.

The prohibition against graven images is, ultimately, a prohibition against the worship of the self. For every graven image, every reductionist model, is a creation of the human mind. To worship the image is to worship our own capacity to understand, to model, to control. It is to place the human intellect on the throne that belongs only to God. The Second Commandment calls us to a higher and more humble path. It calls us to lift our eyes from our maps, however beautiful and detailed they may be, and to gaze with wonder at the vast, mysterious, and glorious territory of a world that points beyond itself to the one who made it.

The Test: Identifying Your Graven Images

If the First Commandment gave us a diagnostic question—"What do I think about most?"—the Second Commandment offers a complementary one: "What model of reality am I unwilling to question?" Where do you experience cognitive closure, that "seize and freeze" response that Kruglanski described? What beliefs do you hold so tightly that contradictory evidence doesn't just fail to convince you, but actually makes you angry? What map have you mistaken for the territory?

For some, it might be a scientific worldview that has hardened into scientism, a refusal to acknowledge that there might be more to reality than what can be measured in a laboratory. For others, it might be a political ideology that has become so central to their identity that they can no longer engage charitably with those who disagree. For still others, it might be a carefully curated image of themselves, a personal brand that they protect and defend at all costs, even when it diverges wildly from who they actually are.

The graven images we worship are often invisible to us precisely because we worship them. They are the water we swim in, the air we breathe. They are so fundamental to how we see the world that we don't see them at all. This is why the Second Commandment is so important. It forces us to step back, to examine our own thinking, to ask ourselves whether we have confused our maps for the territory. It calls us to a posture of perpetual self-examination, not out of neurotic self-doubt, but out of a humble recognition that we are finite beings trying to understand an infinite reality.

One practical way to identify your graven images is to pay attention to your emotional reactions. When you encounter an idea that contradicts your worldview, how do you respond? Do you feel curious, eager to understand a different perspective? Or do you feel threatened, angry, defensive? The latter response is often a sign that you have encountered a challenge to one of your graven images. The map you have been worshipping is being questioned, and your instinct is to protect it. This is a moment of opportunity. It is a chance to ask yourself: "Am I defending the territory, or am I defending my map of the territory? Am I seeking truth, or am I seeking to be right?"

Another diagnostic is to examine what you cannot imagine being wrong about. What beliefs are so central to your sense of self that if they were proven false, you would feel as though your entire worldview had collapsed? These are your graven images. They are the maps you have elevated to the status of territory. The Second Commandment does not call you to abandon these beliefs, but it does call you to hold them with humility, to acknowledge that they are human constructions, and to remain open to the possibility that the territory might be richer and more complex than your map suggests.

The Christian faith itself provides a powerful example of this principle. Christianity makes bold, specific claims about the nature of reality, about God, about Jesus Christ, about sin and redemption. These are not vague, feel-good platitudes; they are concrete assertions about the territory. But Christianity, at its best, also insists that God is transcendent, that He cannot be fully captured by any human theology, that our understanding is always "through a glass, darkly." The creeds and doctrines of the church are maps, essential and valuable maps, but they are not the territory. The territory is the living God Himself, who is always more than we can comprehend. This is why the Second Commandment is so central to the Christian tradition. It is a built-in safeguard against the idolatry of our own understanding, a reminder that we worship not our theology, but the God our theology attempts to describe.

The High Cost of Certainty: From Conviction to Radicalisation

What happens when our devotion to a map becomes absolute? The initial comfort of cognitive closure gives way to something far more dangerous. The emotional anger we feel when our map is questioned is a symptom of a deeper process, one that psychologists refer to as **cognitive dissonance**. When we are presented with evidence that contradicts a deeply held belief—especially one tied to our identity or moral framework—we experience a profound mental discomfort. We have two choices: either update our map (our belief) to accommodate the new information from the territory, or reject the territory and double down on the map.

For the idolater, the choice is always the latter. Rejecting the map would mean admitting they were wrong, which is psychologically painful. More than that, it would mean abandoning the certainty and security the map provides. So, they engage in ever-more-extreme forms of motivated reasoning to protect their graven image. They don't just ignore contradictory evidence; they actively reinterpret it as proof of a conspiracy against them. The person who questions their map is no longer just mistaken; they are malicious, part of an evil out-group seeking to destroy the truth. This is the psychological pathway from conviction to extremism.

This process is supercharged in the echo chambers of the internet. As researchers like John T. Jost have detailed, our cognitive and motivational systems are deeply intertwined with our social identities. We are driven by powerful **ego-justifying** and **group-justifying** motives, which compel us to defend not only our own beliefs but also the beliefs of our in-group. When we are immersed in an online community that shares our map, any challenge from the outside is perceived as an attack on the entire group. The algorithm feeds us a constant stream of content that reinforces our shared map, while social dynamics punish any deviation from the consensus. The result is a powerful feedback loop. The more we invest in the group's map, the more dissonance we feel when confronted with reality, and the more we retreat into the echo chamber for validation. The map becomes a shared idol, a banner under which the group unites against a hostile world.

We see this process at work in the political sphere with devastating consequences. As affective polarisation—the tendency to view opposing partisans as morally repugnant—intensifies, people are no longer disagreeing about policy; they are fighting a holy war against evil. Their political ideology has ceased to be a map for navigating the complexities of governance and has become a graven image demanding total devotion. This is how ordinary, decent people can become radicalised. They begin with a legitimate desire for a better world, but they fall in love with a particular map for achieving it. They surround themselves with others who worship the same map. And when the territory proves more complex than their map allows, they conclude that the territory—and anyone who defends it—must be corrupt.

This is not a new phenomenon. The history of religious wars, totalitarian movements, and genocides is a history of graven images. The Nazi ideology was a grotesque racial map of humanity. The communist project was a rigid economic map of society. In both cases, the map was elevated to the status of absolute truth, and any part of the territory—any human being—that did not fit the map was eliminated. The Second Commandment is a bulwark against this horror. It is a recognition that whenever a finite, human-made system is elevated to the status of the ultimate, the result is not enlightenment, but bloodshed.

Living in the Tension: The Way of Humility

How, then, are we to live? If all our beliefs are just maps, does that mean there is no truth? If all our models are incomplete, does that mean we can't know anything for certain? This is the nihilistic trap that the modern mind often falls into when confronted with the limits of its own understanding. But the Second Commandment does not lead to nihilism; it leads to humility.

It does not ask us to abandon our maps. We need them to live. We need scientific theories, political convictions, and theological doctrines. What it forbids is *worshipping* them. It calls us to hold our beliefs with a certain posture: one of conviction and humility, of confidence and openness. It is the posture of the true scientist, who is committed to their theory but is always looking for the data that will refine or even overturn it. It is the posture of the wise statesman, who fights for their principles but is always willing to listen to the other side. It is the posture of the mature believer, who cherishes their tradition but knows that the God they worship cannot be contained within it.

Living this way means embracing tension. It means accepting that we can be committed to a belief while also acknowledging its limitations. It means having the courage to act on our convictions while also having the humility to admit that we might be wrong. It means defining ourselves not by the certainty of our maps, but by our commitment to the search for the territory. This is a difficult path to walk. It is far easier to retreat into the false certainty of a graven image, to find a tribe that worships the same idol, and to declare war on everyone else. But the path of humility is the only path to wisdom. It is the only path that keeps us in contact with reality. And it is the only path that allows for grace, for dialogue, and for the possibility of a shared future.

The ultimate answer to the problem of graven images is not to have no images, but to have the right one. The Christian faith makes a radical claim: that the transcendent, unmappable God has, in one singular instance, made Himself known in a concrete, historical person. It claims that Jesus Christ is not another map, but the territory itself, the Word made flesh. This is a claim that must be investigated, not simply accepted. But it offers a solution to the dilemma of the Second Commandment. It suggests that we can have a concrete object for our worship that is not a reductionist idol, but the true image of the invisible God. And in orienting our lives around that image, we are not closing ourselves off from reality, but opening ourselves up to it in all its fullness.

Chapter 3: Lex Integritatis - The Law of Integrity

You shall not take the name of the LORD your God in vain, for the LORD will not hold him guiltless who takes his name in vain. (Exodus 20:7)

In 2003, a 19-year-old Stanford dropout named Elizabeth Holmes founded a company that would, for a time, captivate Silicon Valley and the world. The company was Theranos, and its promise was nothing short of revolutionary. Holmes claimed to have invented a technology that could run hundreds of diagnostic tests—from cholesterol levels to complex genetic analyses—from a single, tiny drop of blood pricked from a finger. She called her device the "Edison." It was a sleek, black box that would, she promised, democratise healthcare, making it accessible, affordable, and painless for everyone. Dressed in her signature black turtleneck, consciously emulating Steve Jobs, Holmes spoke with an unnerving, wide-eyed conviction. Her words painted a picture of a future where every home could have a Theranos device, where diseases could be detected in their earliest stages, and where millions of lives would be saved.

Her speech was powerful. It was more than just descriptive; it was creative. It conjured a new reality, and people desperately wanted to live in it. Esteemed venture capitalists, seasoned politicians, and corporate titans lined up to invest. The Theranos board swelled with luminaries, including former U.S. Secretaries of State George Shultz and Henry Kissinger. At its peak, the company was valued at over $9 billion, and Holmes, with a net worth of $4.5 billion, was crowned by *Forbes* as the youngest self-made female billionaire in history. She had spoken a new world into existence.

There was just one problem. The world she had spoken of was a lie. The Edison machine never worked. The revolutionary technology was a fiction. Internally, the company was in a state of chaos, using commercially available, off-the-shelf machines from other companies to run the tests it claimed to be performing with its own proprietary technology. The few tests it did run on its own devices were wildly inaccurate. Yet, for years, Holmes and her second-in-command, Sunny Balwani, continued to speak as if their fictional world was real. They lied to investors, to partners, to doctors, and to the public. They used words not to describe reality, but to obscure it, to manipulate it, and to create a mirage that enriched and empowered them.

In 2015, the mirage began to dissolve. A series of investigative articles by *Wall Street Journal* reporter John Carreyrou exposed the massive fraud. The gap between the world Holmes had described and the actual, existing world was revealed to be a chasm. The fallout was catastrophic. The company that had been valued at $9 billion collapsed into nothing. Investors lost everything. But the most significant loss was not financial; it was a loss of trust. The doctors who had partnered with Theranos, the patients who had received faulty test results, the investors who had believed in the vision—all experienced a profound sense of betrayal. The words that had built an empire had been exposed as empty, and in the process, they had poisoned a well of social trust that is far more valuable than any amount of capital.

Elizabeth Holmes had broken the Third Commandment. Not in the sense of using a swear word, but in the most profound sense imaginable. She had invoked a sacred name—the name of truth, of healing, of a better future—and she had used it in vain, to serve her own ends. Elizabeth had demonstrated, on a global stage, the catastrophic consequences of detaching language from reality. Her story is a modern parable of a timeless law: when truth becomes a tool, social cohesion dissolves.

Words That Build Worlds

"You shall not take the name of the LORD your God in vain." For most of modern history, this commandment has been relegated to the realm of personal piety, interpreted as a simple prohibition against blasphemy or using "God" as a curse word. But this is a shallow reading of a deeply profound psychological and sociological principle. The ancient Hebrews understood something about language that modern society is painfully rediscovering: words do not just describe the world; they create it. The name of God, in their worldview, represented the ultimate reality, the foundational principle of existence itself. To take that name "in vain"—the Hebrew word, *shav*, means empty, hollow, or false—was to use the language of ultimate reality in a way that was disconnected from truth. It was to make a promise you had no intention of keeping, to swear an oath you would not honour, to invoke a sacred value for a profane purpose. It was, in short, to lie in a way that corroded the very fabric of society.

In the mid-20th century, the Oxford philosopher J.L. Austin stumbled upon this ancient insight. He noticed that some sentences don't seem to describe reality at all, but rather to *do* something. When a judge says, "I sentence you to ten years in prison," they are not describing a state of affairs; they are creating one. When two people say, "I do," at a wedding, they are not reporting on their marital status; they are changing it. Austin called these **performative utterances**. They are speech acts that, when spoken in the right context by the right person, alter social reality. You cannot make a promise without saying the words, "I promise." You cannot appoint someone to a position without saying, "I appoint you." Our social and institutional worlds are built and sustained by these performative speech acts.

Austin realised that while descriptive statements (which he called **constative**) are judged by whether they are true or false, performative utterances are judged by a different standard: whether they are **felicitous** or **infelicitous**. That is, whether they succeed or fail in doing what they set out to do. For a performative to be felicitous, certain conditions must be met. The person speaking must have the authority to perform the act (a random person on the street cannot sentence you to prison), the circumstances must be appropriate (you can't christen a ship that's already been christened), and, crucially, the speaker must have the appropriate intentions and must follow through on the act. If you say, "I promise to pay you back," but you have no intention of doing so, your speech act is infelicitous. It is a hollow promise, a vain use of language. You have taken the sacred name of "promise" in vain.

The Third Commandment, then, can be understood as a law about the felicity of our most important speech acts. It is a command to ensure that our words are not empty, that they are backed by intention, commitment, and reality. It is a recognition that a society in which promises are meaningless, in which oaths are broken, in which declarations are false, is a society that will inevitably collapse. Trust is the invisible thread that holds a society together, and that thread is woven from felicitous speech acts. Every time we use language in vain, we snip one of those threads.

The Neuroscience of Broken Promises

This ancient religious and philosophical insight is now being confirmed by modern neuroscience. Our brains are wired for trust. The act of trusting and being trusted is mediated by a powerful neurochemical: **oxytocin**. When someone places their trust in us, our brains release oxytocin, which in turn motivates us to act in a trustworthy manner. When we trust someone else, oxytocin reduces our innate fear of social betrayal, allowing us to cooperate and form bonds. Paul Zak, a pioneer in the field of neuroeconomics, has called oxytocin the "moral molecule." His research has shown that high-trust societies and organisations are more prosperous, more innovative, and more fulfilling to live in. Trust is the secret sauce of social cohesion and economic prosperity.

But what happens in the brain when that trust is violated? It triggers what neuroscientists call a **social prediction error**. Our brains are constantly making predictions about the world, including the social world. Based on someone's words and past actions, we form a model of their intentions. When they say, "I'll be there for you," our brain predicts that they will, in fact, be there for us. When they fail to show up, that prediction is violated. This error signal is registered in the brain with a jolt of negative emotion. It feels like a threat, a betrayal. The oxytocin-fueled sense of connection is replaced by the stress hormones cortisol and adrenaline. The neural networks that support cooperation are shut down, and the ones that govern vigilance and self-protection are activated.

This is the neurological reality of having the name taken in vain. When a politician promises to serve the public but is caught serving their own interests, it creates a massive social prediction error. When a company runs advertisements celebrating its commitment to the environment while secretly polluting, it generates a wave of cynicism and distrust. When a friend swears they will keep a secret and then broadcasts it, the feeling of betrayal is a tangible, physiological event. Each of these is an infelicitous speech act. The words were spoken, but they were empty, hollow, vain. And the result is a degradation of trust, not just in that individual or institution, but in the very language they used. The sacred names—"public service," "sustainability," "friendship"—become tarnished, and we become less likely to trust them in the future.

The Modern Sins of Speech

Our modern world has become a factory for infelicitous speech acts. We are drowning in a sea of language that has been detached from reality, used not to communicate truth but to manipulate, to signal status, and to gain power. The Third Commandment has never been more relevant, or more widely violated.

The Idol of Political Spin

Political language has always been prone to exaggeration and evasion. But in the contemporary landscape, it has often devolved into a pure exercise in what has been called **post-truth** politics. This is not just about lying; it is about a complete indifference to the truth. It is a worldview in which language is not a tool for describing reality, but a weapon for creating it. A politician says something that is demonstrably false. When confronted with the evidence, they do not retract the statement; they repeat it, more loudly. They are not trying to win an argument; they are trying to bend reality to their will. They are using language to create a tribal identity, to signal to their followers that they are on the same team, a team that is defined by its rejection of the "mainstream" or "elite" version of reality. The words themselves cease to have any stable meaning; their only function is to signal loyalty.

This is a catastrophic violation of the Third Commandment. It takes the sacred name of public discourse—the shared language we use to debate our common future—and uses it in vain. It creates a constant stream of social prediction errors, to the point where citizens become so cynical that they cease to believe anything a politician says. Trust in government, in institutions, and in the media plummets. Without a shared foundation of trust and a common understanding of reality, a society cannot solve its problems. It dissolves into warring tribes, each with its own private language and its own private reality. Social cohesion becomes impossible.

The Idol of Corporate Virtue Signalling

A similar phenomenon has taken over the corporate world. In an age where consumers and employees increasingly expect companies to have a social conscience, many corporations have responded not by fundamentally changing their behaviour, but by changing their language. This is the world of **corporate virtue signalling**. A fossil fuel company will launch a multi-million dollar advertising campaign about its investment in renewable energy, while the vast majority of its capital expenditure remains in oil and gas exploration. A fast-fashion brand will release a "conscious collection" made from recycled materials, while its core business model continues to rely on exploitative labour practices and environmental degradation. A bank will publicly celebrate Pride Month with rainbow logos and parade floats, while simultaneously funding political candidates who actively work to undermine LGBTQ+ rights.

In each case, the language of morality—"sustainability," "diversity," "empowerment"—is being taken in vain. It is being used not as a genuine commitment to ethical action, but as a marketing tool, a way to manage public perception and attract customers. This is an infelicitous speech act on a massive scale. The companies are making a promise—"We are a good and ethical company"—that they have no intention of keeping. The result, once again, is the erosion of trust. As consumers become more aware of this hypocrisy, they become cynical about all corporate attempts to engage in moral discourse. The very language of corporate social responsibility becomes devalued, making it harder for genuinely ethical companies to distinguish themselves. The name of "virtue" is taken in vain, and everyone suffers.

The Idol of Moral Grandstanding

The same dynamic plays out at the individual level, particularly on social media. Philosophers Justin Tosi and Brandon Warmke have identified a specific type of discourse they call **moral grandstanding**. This is the use of moral talk for the primary purpose of self-promotion. The grandstander is not trying to contribute to a genuine ethical conversation; they are trying to impress others with their own moral purity. They use public forums to broadcast their outrage, to condemn others, and to signal their allegiance to the "correct" side of an issue. Their goal is not to persuade, but to gain status within their in-group.

Research by psychologists like Joshua Grubbs has shown that moral grandstanding is closely linked to narcissistic traits. People who engage in it are often more interested in dominance and status than in the moral issues they are discussing. And, crucially, their public pronouncements often do not correlate with their private behaviour. They talk a good game, but they don't live it out. They are, in the most literal sense, taking the name of morality in vain.

This has a toxic effect on public discourse. It turns conversations about important ethical issues into a performance, a competition for who can sound the most virtuous. It encourages extremism, as people try to outdo each other in their displays of moral fervour. And it breeds cynicism, as people come to see all moral talk as a disingenuous status game. The sacred language we need to navigate complex ethical dilemmas becomes a weapon in a petty social competition. The name of "justice" or "compassion" is hollowed out, leaving us with only the empty performance of virtue.

The Law of Integrity

The Third Commandment is not a quaint prohibition against swearing. It is a fundamental law of social reality, a Law of Integrity. It is a command to maintain the sacred link between our words and our world. It insists that our promises must be kept, that our oaths must be honoured, and that our declarations must be true. It is a recognition that language is not a toy to be played with, but a powerful tool for building—or destroying—worlds.

When we take the name of God, or truth, or justice, or love, in vain, we are not just performing an infelicitous speech act. We are committing an act of social vandalism. We are chipping away at the foundations of trust upon which our entire civilisation is built. The cynicism, polarisation, and institutional decay we see all around us are the predictable consequences of a society that has forgotten this law. We have become a culture of Elizabeth Holmeses, big and small, using language to create false realities, and we are now living in the rubble of their collapse.

To obey the Third Commandment is to commit to a life of integrity. It is to commit to saying what we mean and meaning what we say. It is to understand that our words have power, and to wield that power with reverence and responsibility. It is to recognise that the name of God—the ultimate reality, the ground of all being and all truth—is not a tool to be used for our own selfish ends. It is the standard to which our own speech must conform. In a world drowning in empty words, the path to restoration begins with a simple, radical, and ancient commitment: to speak the truth, to live the truth, and to never, ever, take the name of the Lord our God in vain.

Let's delve deeper into the mechanics of this decay, examining the specific ways in which our modern world has turned the abuse of language into an industrial-scale enterprise.

The Anatomy of Political Spin: The Case of the 'Ironclad' Promise

Consider the case of Australian politics. In the lead-up to the 2013 federal election, the then-opposition leader, Tony Abbott, sought to neutralise a potent political attack from the incumbent Labor government. Labor claimed that Abbott, if elected, would make deep cuts to education, health, and public broadcasting. To counter this, Abbott deployed a series of powerful performative utterances. He stood before the nation and declared, "No cuts to education, no cuts to health, no change to pensions, no change to the GST, and no cuts to the ABC or SBS." It was not a suggestion or a hope; it was framed as an absolute, unconditional promise. He used the word "ironclad" to describe his commitment.

This was a felicitous speech act in its initial performance. Abbott was the leader of the opposition, a person with the authority to make such a promise about his party's intentions. The circumstances were appropriate—an election campaign. The words were clear and direct. The public, hearing this, formed a social prediction: if this man is elected, these specific areas will be protected. For many voters, this promise was a decisive factor in their decision.

After winning the election, however, the 2014 budget handed down by his government contained what were widely described as significant cuts or funding changes to all of those areas. The government argued that they were not "cuts" but "savings" or "efficiency dividends." They engaged in a protracted semantic debate, attempting to redefine the meaning of the words they had used. But for the public, the social prediction had been violated. The promise, which had seemed so solid, was revealed to be hollow. The word "ironclad" had rusted away to nothing.

The neurological and social fallout was immense. The government's polling numbers collapsed and never fully recovered. The term "ironclad" became a national joke, a synonym for a political lie. But the damage went far deeper than the fortunes of one political party. It created a lasting social prediction error in the Australian electorate. It taught a generation of voters that even the most emphatic, seemingly unambiguous promises from political leaders could not be trusted. The sacred name of a political promise was taken in vain, and the entire political system was diminished as a result. The cynicism that followed was not an irrational mood; it was a rational response to a profound betrayal of trust.

The Greenwashing Machine: Volkswagen's 'Clean Diesel' Deception

The corporate world offers an even more egregious example in the Volkswagen emissions scandal, a case study in industrial-scale virtue signalling. In the mid-2000s, Volkswagen launched a major marketing campaign in the United States for its new line of "Clean Diesel" cars. The company's advertisements were a masterclass in performative utterance. They promised a car that was not only powerful and fuel-efficient but also environmentally friendly. They invoked the sacred name of "green" technology. One ad featured a series of old, polluting cars being disqualified from a race, leaving only the virtuous VW diesel. The message was clear: by buying a Volkswagen, you were not just buying a car; you were making an ethical choice, a contribution to a cleaner planet.

This was a powerful and successful campaign. Volkswagen's sales in the US surged. Consumers believed they were doing the right thing. They had formed a social prediction based on the company's explicit promises. But in 2015, the Environmental Protection Agency (EPA) revealed the shocking truth. Volkswagen had deliberately programmed its diesel engines with a "defeat device." This software could detect when the car was being tested, and only then would it turn on the full emissions controls. In normal road use, the cars were emitting nitrogen oxides at up to 40 times the legal limit in the United States.

The company had not just bent the rules; it had built a sophisticated, global conspiracy to lie. The name "Clean Diesel" was not just marketing spin; it was a hollow, cynical falsehood. The speech act was profoundly infelicitous. The betrayal was staggering. The company paid billions in fines, recalled millions of cars, and its CEO was forced to resign. But again, the greatest damage was to the fabric of trust. The scandal tainted the entire automotive industry. It made consumers deeply skeptical of all environmental claims made by corporations. The name "clean" had been used to perpetrate a dirty trick, and the very concept of corporate environmental responsibility was devalued in the process.

The Digital Pillory: Moral Grandstanding and Public Shaming

Nowhere is the temptation to take a name in vain more potent than on social media, the global stage for moral performance. Consider the case of Justine Sacco. In 2013, Sacco, a corporate communications director, was on a flight from New York to South Africa. Before takeoff, she tweeted to her 170 followers: "Going to Africa. Hope I don't get AIDS. Just kidding. I'm white!" It was, by all accounts, a bad joke. An attempt at edgy, satirical humour that failed spectacularly. It was clumsy, offensive, and ignorant.

By the time her plane landed 11 hours later, her life had been destroyed. Her tweet had been discovered by a journalist, retweeted, and had gone viral. The hashtag #HasJustineLandedYet was the number one trending topic worldwide. Tens of thousands of people, who had never met her and knew nothing about her, descended upon her with a torrent of righteous fury. They condemned her as a racist, a monster. They demanded she be fired. Her employer, facing a public relations firestorm, quickly complied. She was fired while she was still in the air.

This was a classic case of moral grandstanding. For the vast majority of people piling on, the goal was not to engage in a nuanced conversation about race, privilege, or the history of AIDS in Africa. The goal was to signal their own virtue. By condemning Justine Sacco, they were performing their own goodness for their followers. "I am not like her," their retweets and comments implicitly declared. "I am on the right side of history. I am a good person." They were using the sacred name of "anti-racism" not to build a better world, but to build their own social status. It was a massive, collective, and infelicitous speech act.

The harm was immense. A person's life was ruined over a single, ill-conceived tweet. But the broader harm was to the quality of our moral discourse. The episode taught millions of people that the digital public square is not a place for good-faith conversation, but a battlefield for moral purity contests. It showed that the slightest misstep could lead to total social annihilation. It encouraged a culture of fear, where people are afraid to speak their minds or ask honest questions for fear of being the next target of the mob. The name of justice was used to perpetrate a cruel and disproportionate punishment, and in the process, the possibility of genuine dialogue and forgiveness was extinguished.

(In perhaps the ultimate example of the exploitative nature of these behaviours, someone else had appropriated her X handle (@JustineSacco), and now 'virtuously' posts about racial, social and economic justice under her name.)

The Way of Integrity: Re-anchoring Words to Worlds

How do we find our way back from this post-truth wilderness? How do we begin to repair the shattered foundations of trust? The Third Commandment does not just diagnose the problem; it points to the solution. The solution is to re-anchor our words to reality. The solution is integrity.

Integrity is not about being perfect. It is about being whole. The word itself comes from the same root as "integer"—a whole number. A person of integrity is a person whose words and actions are integrated, whose public pronouncements match their private convictions, whose promises are backed by their performance. To live with integrity is to consciously and consistently strive to make our speech acts felicitous.

This means, first, a commitment to speaking truthfully, even when it is difficult. It means resisting the temptation to use language as a weapon, to spin, to exaggerate, or to mislead. It means valuing the accurate description of reality more than we value winning an argument or scoring a political point.

Second, it means a commitment to keeping our promises. It means not saying "I will" unless we genuinely intend to, and then doing everything in our power to follow through. It means understanding that a promise is a sacred act, a creation of a new moral reality, and that to break it is to do violence to that reality.

Third, it means a commitment to humility in our moral pronouncements. It means resisting the urge to engage in moral grandstanding, to use ethical language as a tool for self-promotion. It means recognising that virtue is demonstrated not by the volume of our condemnations, but by the quiet consistency of our own character. It means being more concerned with being good than with looking good.

Ultimately, the Third Commandment points us back to the First. The name we are forbidden to take in vain is the name of the LORD our God. This is because, in the biblical worldview, God is the ultimate reality, the ground of all truth. To take His name in vain is the ultimate act of detaching language from reality. Conversely, to revere His name is to revere truth itself. To orient our lives around a transcendent God who is truth, and who demands truth from his followers, is the ultimate anchor against the shifting tides of post-truth culture. It provides a standard outside of ourselves, our tribe, and our political party to which our speech must be accountable.

In a world drowning in empty words, the path to restoration begins with a simple, radical, and ancient commitment: to speak the truth, to live the truth, and to never, ever, take the name of the Lord our God in vain.

To fully grasp the radical nature of this command, we must place it in its historical context. In the ancient Near East, the gods were often seen as capricious and transactional. Oaths were sworn in their names not as a commitment to truth, but as a form of magic. By invoking a powerful deity, one hoped to bind reality to one's words, to force an outcome. The names of the gods were tools to be manipulated for personal gain. The God of the Hebrew Bible, however, is different. He is not a tool to be used, but the ultimate reality to which one must conform. His name is not a magic word, but the embodiment of truth and order. The Third Commandment, therefore, was a revolutionary statement. It was a declaration that the foundation of this new society was not to be power, or magic, or manipulation, but integrity. It was a command to align the human world of speech with the divine reality of truth.

This commitment to integrity has profound psychological consequences. When our words and actions are aligned, we experience a sense of inner coherence and peace. Psychologists call this **cognitive consistency**. When our words and actions are misaligned—when we say one thing and do another—we experience **cognitive dissonance**, a state of internal conflict and stress. This is the unease you feel when you tell a lie, the guilt that gnaws at you when you break a promise. It is the psychological price of taking a name in vain. A life of integrity is not just a moral good; it is a psychological necessity. It is the only way to live in harmony with ourselves, with others, and with reality itself.

In our modern world, we have created a culture that actively encourages cognitive dissonance. We are constantly pressured to present a curated, idealized version of ourselves on social media, a version that often bears little resemblance to our actual lives. We are incentivized to engage in moral grandstanding, to perform our virtue for an audience, even if our private actions do not match our public pronouncements. We are surrounded by political and corporate leaders who model a cynical and manipulative use of language. In such an environment, it is easy to become cynical ourselves, to conclude that integrity is a naive ideal, that everyone is just playing a game. But the psychological cost of this cynicism is immense. It leads to a sense of alienation, of meaninglessness, of being disconnected from reality. We become hollow men and women, our words as empty as the promises of a fraudulent tech CEO.

The path back is the path of integrity. It is the difficult, daily work of striving for cognitive consistency. It is the small acts of telling the truth when a lie would be easier, of keeping a promise when it is inconvenient, of admitting when we are wrong instead of doubling down. It is the conscious decision to value truth more than social status, to value character more than reputation. It is the recognition that our words are not just sounds we make, but the very building blocks of our reality. And it is the understanding that the most important name we can ever hope to honour is the name of truth itself.

Chapter 4: Lex Aequilibrii - The Law of Balance

> *Remember the Sabbath day, to keep it holy. Six days you shall labour, and do all your work, but the seventh day is a Sabbath to the LORD your God. On it you shall not do any work, you, or your son, or your daughter, your male servant, or your female servant, or your livestock, or the sojourner who is within your gates. For in six days the LORD made heaven and earth, the sea, and all that is in them, and rested on the seventh day. Therefore the LORD blessed the Sabbath day and made it holy. (Exodus 20:8-11)*

In the early 1990s, a young neuroscientist named Marcus Raichle was working at Washington University in St. Louis, using the then-new technology of positron emission tomography (PET) to peer inside the working human brain. The logic of these early brain imaging studies was simple and elegant. You would have a person lie in the scanner and perform a specific mental task—looking at pictures, solving a puzzle, reading words—and you would measure the corresponding increase in blood flow to different brain regions. Then, as a baseline for comparison, you would have them do nothing at all, simply rest with their eyes closed or stare at a blank cross on a screen. The assumption, which seemed perfectly logical, was that the brain at rest was a brain doing nothing, a clean slate against which the activity of a focused, working brain could be measured.

But Raichle and his colleagues kept noticing something strange, a persistent and puzzling anomaly in their data. There was a network of brain regions that behaved in the exact opposite way to what they expected. When a person was engaged in a demanding external task, these regions became quiet, their activity suppressed. But the moment the task ended and the person was told to "rest," this network roared to life. It was as if the brain, when freed from the demands of the outside world, immediately defaulted to a different, and surprisingly active, mode of operation. For years, this was treated as noise in the data, an inconvenient quirk to be statistically removed. But Raichle began to suspect it was something more. What if "rest" wasn't the absence of activity, but a different *kind* of activity? What if the brain at rest was actually hard at work on something important?

In 2001, Raichle's team published a landmark paper that gave this mysterious network a name: the **Default Mode Network** (DMN). The discovery revolutionised neuroscience. It revealed that the brain at rest is not idle at all. Instead, it is engaged in a host of vital, internally focused tasks: consolidating memories, making sense of our experiences, reflecting on our past and imagining our future, understanding the minds of others, and constructing our very sense of self. The DMN, it turns out, is the architect of our internal world, the weaver of the narrative of our lives. And it can only do its work when we stop, when we disengage from the constant stream of external demands and allow our minds to wander, to reflect, and to be still.

This discovery, born from the sterile environment of a brain scanner, is a stunning modern confirmation of an ancient and sacred law, one that has been largely dismissed by the modern world as an archaic and inconvenient restriction. The Fourth Commandment, to "remember the Sabbath day, to keep it holy," is not a call to idleness or a quaint religious observance. It is a profound psychological and biological necessity, a command to protect the very machinery of meaning-making in our brains. It is a recognition that a culture that never stops, that sees rest as a weakness and productivity as the ultimate virtue, is a culture that will, inevitably, break. It will break its minds, its bodies, and its social fabric. The law of rhythm is not a suggestion; it is a fundamental operating principle of our humanity.

The Tyranny of the Task-Positive

To understand the significance of the Default Mode Network, we must first understand its opposite. Neuroscientists refer to the brain systems that are active during externally focused, goal-oriented tasks as the **Task-Positive Network** (TPN). This is the network you are using right now to read these words. It is the network of focus, of attention, of problem-solving. It is the part of your brain that gets things done. For most of human history, the TPN was engaged for specific periods of activity—hunting, farming, building—followed by natural periods of rest, where the DMN could take over.

But the modern world has declared war on rest. We live in a culture of **hustle**, a relentless, 24/7 assault on the very idea of stopping. Our smartphones, our constant companions, are portals to an infinite stream of external demands: emails, notifications, news alerts, social media updates. We have created an "always-on" environment that keeps our Task-Positive Network in a state of chronic activation. We work longer hours, we check our email in bed, we scroll through our feeds while waiting in line. We have come to see any moment of unstructured, unproductive time as a waste. We have tied our very identity and self-worth to our output:

> "I am busy, therefore I am."

This relentless focus on the external comes at a tremendous cost. It is a form of self-imposed cognitive starvation. By keeping our TPN constantly engaged, we are systematically starving our DMN of the time it needs to do its work. And the consequences are devastating, both for our minds and our bodies.

The Brain on Burnout

When the brain is forced into a state of perpetual external focus, it begins to break down. This is the neurological reality of **burnout**, a state of chronic physical and emotional exhaustion that the World Health Organization now officially recognises as an occupational phenomenon. Burnout is not just "feeling tired." It is a profound state of cognitive depletion. People experiencing burnout report an inability to concentrate, a loss of memory, and a decline in creative problem-solving skills. They feel emotionally numb, cynical, and detached from their work and their relationships. They are, in a very real sense, losing their minds.

This is because the functions that are lost in burnout are precisely the functions that are supported by the Default Mode Network. Without the restorative downtime that allows the DMN to operate, our ability to consolidate memory is impaired. We struggle to learn new things and to recall what we already know. Our ability to make sense of our experiences, to weave them into a coherent narrative, is diminished. We feel lost, adrift, and disconnected from our own life story. Our capacity for empathy and social cognition, also supported by the DMN, begins to fail. We become more irritable, less patient, and less able to understand the perspectives of others. Our relationships suffer. Our creativity plummets. The DMN is the wellspring of novel ideas, the place where our brains make surprising connections between disparate pieces of information. When we don't give it time to wander, we become stuck in rigid, uncreative patterns of thought.

The Body on Overdrive

The damage is not just psychological; it is profoundly physiological. A state of constant work and external focus is a state of chronic stress. Our bodies are not designed for it. The stress response system, governed by the hormone **cortisol**, is designed for short, acute bursts of threat. It prepares the body for fight or flight. But when that system is activated day after day, week after week, the results are catastrophic. Chronically elevated cortisol levels wreak havoc on the body. They suppress the immune system, making us more vulnerable to infections. They disrupt our metabolism, leading to weight gain and an increased risk of diabetes. They raise our blood pressure, increasing the risk of heart disease and stroke. A culture of overwork is a culture of chronic illness.

Nowhere is this more evident than in the modern epidemic of sleep deprivation. Sleep is the ultimate Sabbath, the most profound period of rest and restoration for both the brain and the body. It is during sleep, particularly the deep, slow-wave stage, that the brain's glymphatic system, its waste-clearance mechanism, is most active, flushing out the toxic byproducts of neural activity that accumulate during the day. It is during sleep that the DMN works in concert with the hippocampus to consolidate memories, transferring them from short-term to long-term storage. And it is during sleep that the immune system does some of its most important work.

Research by scientists like Luciana Besedovsky has shown that sleep is crucial for the formation of **immunological memory**. When we are exposed to a pathogen, our immune system learns to recognise and fight it. This "memory" is consolidated during sleep. Studies have shown that people who get a full night's sleep after a vaccination mount a significantly stronger and more lasting antibody response than those who are sleep-deprived. To put it bluntly: a culture that doesn't sleep is a culture that can't fight disease. The Fourth Commandment is a public health mandate.

The Modern Breaches of Rhythm

The modern world has developed a host of practices and technologies that actively wage war against the law of balance. These are not just bad habits; they are systemic failures that push us towards a state of perpetual, unsustainable activity.

The Cult of Hustle: A Case Study in Exhaustion

Consider the story of Miya, a composite character drawn from dozens of real-life accounts of burnout in the tech industry. Miya joined a fast-growing startup in her mid-twenties, full of ambition and a genuine belief in the company's mission. The culture was intoxicating. The office was filled with beanbags, free snacks, and a palpable sense of changing the world. The unofficial motto, plastered on posters and repeated in meetings, was "Work hard, play hard." But in reality, there was only work. The "play" was just more work in a different setting—team-building exercises that ran late into the night, weekend "hackathons" that were mandatory in all but name.

Miya bought into the hustle completely. She worked 12-hour days, answered emails at 2 a.m., and prided herself on being the first one in and the last one out. Her identity became fused with her job. Her productivity was her self-worth. She was rewarded for her dedication with promotions and praise. But slowly, insidiously, things began to unravel. She started forgetting things—important deadlines, conversations with colleagues. She found it harder and harder to focus, her mind constantly flitting from one task to another. She stopped exercising, stopped seeing friends, stopped calling her family. Her diet consisted of whatever she could grab from the office kitchen. She was constantly tired but couldn't sleep, her mind racing with anxieties about work.

One afternoon, sitting in a meeting, she felt a strange sense of detachment, as if she were watching a movie of her own life. She couldn't follow the conversation. The words sounded like meaningless noise. Later that day, her doctor told her she was suffering from severe burnout. Her cortisol levels were through the roof, her immune system was suppressed, and she was on the verge of a complete physical and mental collapse. Miya's story is not an exception; it is the norm in a culture that has made a religion of overwork. It is the predictable outcome of a society that has forgotten the law of rhythm.

The Always-On Tether: The Case of the Phantom Buzz

Hustle culture is enabled and amplified by our technology. The smartphone is a remarkable tool, but it is also a digital tether, a portable portal to the world of work and external demands that we carry with us at all times. The clear boundary that once existed between the office and the home, between work and rest, has been obliterated. We are now expected to be available at all hours, to respond to emails at night, to join conference calls on weekends. This "always-on" culture creates a state of perpetual low-grade cognitive load. Our brains are never truly at rest, because a part of our attention is always reserved for the possibility of the next notification, the next demand.

This has given rise to a bizarre and uniquely modern phenomenon: the **phantom buzz**. Many people report feeling a vibration in their pocket, a phantom notification from their phone, only to pull it out and find nothing there. This is not a hallucination. It is a sign that the brain has been rewired. It has learned to be in a state of constant, anxious anticipation. The nervous system is so primed for the next digital interruption that it starts to generate the sensation on its own. It is a neurological twitch, a symptom of a brain that has forgotten how to be still.

This constant state of alert has a corrosive effect on our ability to engage in the kind of deep, focused work that produces real value. But more importantly, it has a corrosive effect on our ability to rest. True rest is not just the absence of work; it is the presence of something else. It is the presence of unstructured time, of play, of contemplation, of connection with loved ones, of engagement with the natural world. The always-on tether robs us of this. It fills every empty moment with a distraction, a notification, a task. It prevents our Default Mode Network from ever truly engaging. We become so accustomed to the constant stream of external stimulation that we become afraid of silence, afraid of stillness, afraid of being alone with our own thoughts. We have forgotten how to rest.

The Illusion of Productivity: The Busy-ness Trap

The final and most insidious breach of the law of balance is the modern illusion of productivity itself. We have come to equate activity with accomplishment. We fill our days with meetings, our inboxes with emails, our to-do lists with tasks.

We feel busy, and we mistake that feeling for importance. But much of this activity is what the computer scientist Cal Newport calls "shallow work"—tasks that are non-cognitively demanding, logistical in nature, and create little new value in the world. We spend our days in a frenzy of shallow work, and we feel exhausted at the end of it, but we have often accomplished very little of real substance.

True productivity, the kind that creates lasting value, requires long, uninterrupted periods of deep work, of intense concentration on a single, demanding task. And deep work, paradoxically, requires deep rest. It is in the periods of rest, when the DMN is active, that our brains consolidate what we have learned, make creative connections, and recharge for the next bout of intense effort. A culture that prioritises shallow, constant activity over deep, rhythmic work is a culture that will, ironically, become less productive, less creative, and less innovative over time. The relentless pursuit of productivity, without the balancing rhythm of rest, is ultimately self-defeating. A culture that never stops eventually grinds to a halt.

The Sabbath as Resistance and Restoration

What, then, is the solution? The Fourth Commandment offers a radical and counter-cultural answer: the Sabbath. The Sabbath is not a day off to catch up on errands or binge-watch a television series. It is a day to *remember* and to *keep holy*. It is a conscious, intentional act of resistance against the tyranny of the task-positive and the cult of productivity. It is a deliberate creation of a sanctuary in time, a 24-hour period in which we cease from all work, from all striving, from all doing, and we simply *are*.

To observe the Sabbath is to make a powerful statement about what is ultimate. It is to declare that our value is not in what we produce, but in who we are as beings created in the image of a God who, himself, rested. The commandment is grounded in the story of creation: "For in six days the LORD made heaven and earth… and rested on the seventh day." This is a staggering theological claim. The all-powerful creator of the universe, who does not grow weary or tired, chose to model the rhythm of work and rest. Rest is not a concession to our weakness; it is woven into the very fabric of the cosmos. It is a part of the divine pattern.

To keep the Sabbath holy is to protect this sacred time from the encroachment of the profane world of work and commerce. It means turning off our phones, closing our laptops, and disengaging from the market. It means creating space for the things that the DMN is designed for: contemplation, connection, and creativity. It is a day for long walks in nature, for unhurried meals with family and friends, for prayer and worship, for reading and reflection, for play and for joy. It is a day to remember that we are more than our jobs, more than our productivity, more than our economic function. We are human beings, and we need to rest.

In a world that is burning out, the Sabbath is not a burden, but a gift. It is a lifeline, a weekly reset for our minds, our bodies, and our souls. It is the law of rhythm that protects us from the law of diminishing returns. It is the divinely ordained mechanism for ensuring that our work is fruitful, our creativity is vibrant, our relationships are rich, and our lives are meaningful. A culture that never stops eventually breaks. The Sabbath is the law that keeps us whole.

The Neuroscience of Restoration: What Happens When We Rest

To fully appreciate the necessity of the Sabbath, we must understand what is actually happening in the brain during periods of rest. The Default Mode Network is not a luxury; it is a biological necessity. When we allow our minds to wander, when we disengage from external tasks, the DMN engages in a complex set of processes that are essential for our cognitive and emotional health.

One of the most important functions of the DMN is **memory consolidation**. Throughout the day, as we experience the world, our brains encode vast amounts of information. But this information is initially stored in a fragile, temporary form in the hippocampus, a structure deep in the brain that acts as a kind of short-term memory buffer. For these memories to become stable and long-lasting, they must be transferred to the neocortex, the outer layer of the brain where long-term memories are stored. This process, called **systems consolidation**, happens primarily during rest, and especially during sleep.

During periods of rest, the brain replays recent experiences, strengthening the neural connections that encode them. It is as if the brain is rehearsing what it has learned, cementing it into place. Without adequate rest, this process is disrupted. Memories remain fragile and are easily forgotten. This is why students who cram all night before an exam, depriving themselves of sleep, often perform worse than those who study less but sleep well. The information never makes it from short-term to long-term storage. The Sabbath, in this sense, is not time away from learning; it is the time when learning is completed.

But the DMN does more than just consolidate memories. It also engages in what neuroscientists call **prospection**—the ability to imagine the future. When our minds wander, they often wander forward in time. We imagine possible scenarios, we plan, we anticipate. This is not idle daydreaming; it is a crucial cognitive function. By mentally simulating the future, we can prepare for it, we can make better decisions, and we can set meaningful goals. People who are chronically stressed and overworked often report a loss of this capacity. They feel trapped in an eternal present, unable to imagine a better future. They have lost the ability to hope. This is because their DMN, starved of rest, can no longer perform this essential function.

The DMN is also central to our sense of **self**. It is the network that is active when we reflect on our own thoughts and feelings, when we consider our values and our identity. In his comprehensive review of the DMN, neuroscientist Vinod Menon argues that the network integrates memory, language, and semantic representations to create a coherent "internal narrative" that reflects our individual experiences. This narrative is what we call the self. It is the story we tell ourselves about who we are, where we have been, and where we are going. Without periods of rest, this narrative begins to fragment. We lose our sense of coherence, our sense of meaning. We feel like we are just going through the motions, disconnected from our own lives. The Sabbath is the time when we re-author our story, when we make sense of our experiences and integrate them into a meaningful whole.

Finally, the DMN is essential for **empathy and social cognition**. When we think about other people, when we try to understand their thoughts and feelings, when we imagine what it is like to be in their shoes, we are using our Default Mode Network. This capacity for empathy is what makes us human. It is the foundation of all our relationships, all our communities, all our moral systems. But empathy is not automatic; it requires cognitive resources. It requires the ability to step back from our own immediate concerns and consider the perspective of another. When we are chronically stressed and overworked, when our Task-Positive Network is constantly engaged, we lose this capacity. We become more self-centred, more irritable, more likely to see others as obstacles rather than as fellow human beings. A culture without rest is a culture without empathy. It is a culture that cannot sustain meaningful relationships or a cohesive society.

The Practical Path: Reclaiming Balance

Understanding the neuroscience of rest is one thing; actually implementing it in our lives is another. The modern world makes it extraordinarily difficult to observe a true Sabbath. The pressures are real. The demands are relentless. The technology is seductive. But the commandment is not a suggestion; it is a law, and it is a law written into our very biology. Ignoring it comes at a cost that we can no longer afford to pay. So how do we begin to reclaim the rhythm of rest?

The first step is to recognise that rest is not something we earn through productivity. It is not a reward for a job well done. It is a fundamental human need, as essential as food or water. We must reject the toxic cultural narrative that equates rest with laziness and busyness with virtue. Rest is not the opposite of work; it is the necessary complement to work. Without rest, our work becomes shallow, our creativity dries up, and our productivity plummets. The Sabbath is not a concession to weakness; it is a strategic investment in our long-term effectiveness and well-being.

The second step is to create clear boundaries (reset the balance) between work and rest. This means, practically, turning off our devices. It means setting specific times when we are not available, when we will not check email, when we will not respond to messages. It means communicating these boundaries to our colleagues, our employers, and our families, and holding them firmly. This will feel uncomfortable at first. We will experience anxiety, the fear of missing out, the worry that we are falling behind. But these feelings are symptoms of our addiction to constant activity. They will pass. And on the other side of that discomfort is a profound sense of freedom and peace.

The third step is to fill our Sabbath time with activities that engage the Default Mode Network. This does not mean passive consumption of entertainment. Binge-watching television or scrolling through social media does not activate the DMN; it keeps the Task-Positive Network engaged in a shallow, unfulfilling way. True rest involves activities that allow the mind to wander: long walks in nature, unhurried conversations with loved ones, reading for pleasure, creative hobbies, prayer and meditation, play. These are the activities that allow our brains to do the deep, restorative work that is essential for our humanity.

Finally, and most importantly, we must recover a sense of the sacred. The commandment is not just to rest, but to "keep the Sabbath holy." This means recognising that rest is not just a biological necessity, but a spiritual discipline. It is a time set apart, a time to remember what is ultimate, a time to reconnect with the transcendent. For those of us who believe in God, the Sabbath is a time to worship, to pray, to read scripture, to remember that we are not self-made but created, not autonomous but dependent, not the centre of the universe but part of a much larger story. But even for those who do not share this belief, the principle holds. The Sabbath is a time to step back from the frantic pace of the world and to ask the big questions: What is my life for? What really matters? What kind of person am I becoming? These are the questions that give life meaning, and they can only be asked in the silence and stillness of rest.

The Collective Dimension: A Society That Rests

The Fourth Commandment is not just an individual prescription; it is a social law. It commands rest not only for the individual, but for "your son, or your daughter, your male servant, or your female servant, or your livestock, or the sojourner who is within your gates." This is a radical egalitarian vision. In the ancient world, where slavery was ubiquitous and social hierarchies were rigid, the Sabbath was a weekly declaration that all human beings, regardless of status, have an inherent dignity and a right to rest. Even the animals and the land itself are included in this covenant of rest.

This collective dimension of the Sabbath has profound implications for how we structure our society. A culture that takes the law of rhythm seriously would not glorify overwork or celebrate the entrepreneur who sleeps under their desk. It would not create economic systems that require people to work multiple jobs just to survive. It would not design technologies that keep us perpetually tethered to our work. Instead, it would create structures that protect and promote rest. It would enforce reasonable working hours, mandate paid holidays, and create spaces and times that are free from the demands of commerce. It would recognise that a healthy society is not one where everyone is maximally productive at all times, but one where everyone has the time and space to rest, to reflect, to connect, and to flourish.

The erosion of the Sabbath is not just a personal problem; it is a social crisis. When an entire culture forgets how to rest, the consequences ripple outward. We see it in the epidemic of burnout, in the rising rates of anxiety and depression, in the breakdown of families and communities, in the loss of creativity and innovation, in the decline of civic engagement and social trust. A culture that never stops is a culture that is slowly breaking apart. The Fourth Commandment is not just a gift to individuals; it is a blueprint for a sustainable and humane society.

Conclusion: The Rhythm That Sustains

The discovery of the Default Mode Network is one of the most important findings in modern neuroscience. It has revealed that rest is not the absence of activity, but a different and essential kind of activity. It has shown us that the brain at rest is hard at work, consolidating memories, constructing meaning, imagining the future, understanding others, and building the very sense of self. It has confirmed, with the precision of modern science, what the ancient law of the Sabbath has always proclaimed: rest is not laziness; it is a biological requirement for meaning, creativity, and empathy.

We live in a world that has declared war on rest. We have created a culture of hustle, an always-on environment, and an illusion of productivity that is slowly destroying our minds, our bodies, and our society. But the law of rhythm is not negotiable. It is written into the fabric of our biology and into the structure of the cosmos itself. A culture that never stops eventually breaks. The Fourth Commandment is the divine prescription for a life of sustainable flourishing. It is the law that keeps us whole. In a world burning out, the Sabbath is not a burden. It is a lifeline. It is the rhythm that sustains.

Chapter 5: Lex Honoris - The Law of Honour

> *Honour your father and your mother, that your days may be long in the land that the LORD your God is giving you. (Exodus 20:12)*

In the late 1940s, a quiet revolution began in a London clinic. It didn't involve politics or armies, but something far more fundamental: the bond between a mother and her child. The revolutionary was a British psychiatrist named John Bowlby, and his subjects were a group of troubled and delinquent boys. These weren't just naughty children; they were profoundly damaged. They lied, they stole, and they showed a chilling lack of remorse. In the detached language of the era, they were labelled "affectionless psychopaths."

As Bowlby painstakingly pieced together their life stories, a stark and haunting pattern emerged. These boys, almost without exception, had been robbed of a mother's consistent love. They had been separated from their mothers for long stretches, shunted between foster homes, or raised in the cold, impersonal sterility of institutions. Bowlby began to suspect that their inability to form relationships wasn't a character flaw, but a wound. Their coldness was not a sign of inherent wickedness, but a direct consequence of a broken primary bond.

This was a heretical idea. The prevailing wisdom, from Freudian psychoanalysis to the advice columns in women's magazines, warned that too much maternal affection would spoil a child, creating a weak, dependent, and clingy adult. Bowlby's clinical experience screamed the opposite. He proposed a new theory, one that would eventually upend decades of psychological dogma. The bond between an infant and its primary caregiver—what he termed **attachment**—was not, he argued, a sentimental extra. It was a fundamental biological and psychological necessity, a built-in survival mechanism as vital for our mental health as food and water are for our physical health.

Bowlby's work, later brilliantly expanded and empirically validated by his American colleague Mary Ainsworth, laid the foundation for what we now know as **attachment theory**. It stands today as one of the most robust and influential theories in modern psychology. And in its findings, we discover a stunning scientific affirmation of one of the oldest moral laws in human history: the Fifth Commandment. "Honour your father and your mother" is not a simple injunction to be polite to your elders. It is a profound statement about the very architecture of a healthy human being and a stable society. It is a recognition that the bond between generations is the primary conduit through which wisdom, stability, and psychological well-being are transmitted. A society that honours this bond is a society that can endure. A society that severs it is a society that will, inevitably, lose its way.

The Secure Base: The Launchpad for a Human Life

Mary Ainsworth's genius was to take Bowlby's theory out of the clinic and into the laboratory of everyday life. Through her groundbreaking "Strange Situation" studies, she created a simple, elegant experiment to observe the attachment bond in action. A mother and her one-year-old child would play in a room with some toys. A stranger would enter, the mother would leave for a few minutes, and then she would return. By carefully observing the child's behaviour during these brief separations and reunions, Ainsworth could identify distinct patterns of attachment.

She discovered that a securely attached infant uses its mother as a **secure base** from which to explore the world. When the mother is present, the child feels confident to play, to investigate, to take risks. If the child becomes frightened or distressed, it knows it can return to the mother for comfort and reassurance. The mother's presence doesn't smother the child's independence; it makes it possible. The secure base is not a cage; it is a launchpad.

This simple observation has profound, lifelong implications. The quality of our early attachments shapes our **internal working models**—the unconscious beliefs and expectations we carry with us about ourselves, about others, and about the world. A child with a secure attachment, whose caregivers were consistently responsive and available, develops an internal working model of the world as a generally safe place, of others as trustworthy, and of the self as worthy of love and care. This becomes the foundation for a life of confidence, resilience, and healthy relationships.

Conversely, a child with an insecure attachment—whose caregivers were neglectful, inconsistent, or abusive—develops a very different internal working model. They may come to see the world as a dangerous place, others as unreliable, and the self as unworthy. These children develop coping strategies—avoidance, anxiety, resistance—that may help them survive a difficult childhood, but which often become maladaptive in adulthood, leading to a lifetime of relationship problems, emotional difficulties, and mental health issues. The research is overwhelming: secure attachment in childhood is a powerful predictor of almost every positive life outcome, from academic success and career satisfaction to marital stability and psychological well-being.

To honour our father and mother, then, is to recognise and value this foundational role. It is to acknowledge that the secure base they provided (or should have provided) is the invisible architecture of our lives. It is to understand that the love, care, and consistency we received in our earliest years are not things we can ever repay, but are a gift that we are called to pass on to the next generation. The commandment is not primarily about the feelings of the parents; it is about the psychological flourishing of the children. It is a command to protect the intergenerational transmission of security and trust.

The Great Inheritance: When the Past is Not Dead

The bond between parent and child is not just about psychological security; it is also about the transmission of **cultural inheritance**. Every society is a repository of accumulated wisdom, a vast storehouse of knowledge, values, and practices that have been tested and refined over generations. This is our great inheritance, the collective wisdom of our ancestors. And the primary vehicle for transmitting this inheritance is the family.

In traditional societies, this was understood implicitly. Elders were revered not just because they were old, but because they were living libraries. They held the knowledge of how to hunt, how to farm, how to build, how to heal. They remembered the stories, the songs, the rituals that gave the tribe its identity and its meaning. To dishonour an elder was not just a personal insult; it was an act of cultural vandalism. It was to tear a page out of the book of the tribe's survival.

In a fascinating 2022 thesis, Harvard researcher Leo Saenger analysed over 400 folklore motifs from 1,200 cultures to create a measure of historical attitudes toward the aged. He found that the valuation of elders was directly related to the stability of the environment and the applicability of their experience. In stable societies, where the challenges of one generation were similar to the challenges of the next, elders were highly valued. Their accumulated knowledge was a precious resource. But in societies undergoing rapid change, where the experience of the elders seemed less relevant to the new challenges, respect for them declined.

This finding has profound implications for our own time. We live in an age of unprecedented technological and social change. The world of our parents and grandparents can seem impossibly distant and irrelevant to the challenges we face today. As a result, we have fallen into a state of **historical amnesia**. We have come to believe that the past has nothing to teach us, that all wisdom is new wisdom, that we can and must invent our values from scratch in every generation. This is a form of collective hubris, and it is incredibly dangerous.

When we sever ourselves from the past, we do not become free; we become disoriented. We lose our ability to navigate the future because we have no map, no compass, no memory of the paths that have been tried before. We are like sailors who have thrown their charts overboard, convinced they can navigate the ocean by the light of their own genius. We are destined to repeat the mistakes of the past, because we have forgotten what they were. The Fifth Commandment is a command to remember. It is a command to stay connected to the great inheritance of human wisdom, to value the accumulated knowledge of our ancestors, and to recognise that we are not the first generation to face the challenges of being human.

The Modern Breakdown: A Society Adrift

The modern Western world has, to a terrifying degree, abandoned the law of honour. We have created a society that systematically devalues the elderly, forgets its own history, and celebrates a form of radical individualism that is corrosive to the very idea of intergenerational bonds. The consequences are all around us, in the loneliness of our atomised lives, the confusion of our cultural moment, and the fragility of our social fabric.

The Exile of the Elders

In traditional societies, the elderly remained at the heart of family and community life until their death. They were cared for by their children and grandchildren, and they continued to play a vital role as advisors, storytellers, and caregivers. In the modern West, we have created a system that systematically removes the elderly from our lives. We have outsourced their care to institutions, to nursing homes and assisted living facilities, places that are often sterile, impersonal, and disconnected from the communities in which these elders lived their lives. We have come to see the care of our own parents not as a sacred duty, but as a logistical problem to be managed.

This is not just a tragedy for the elderly, who often experience profound loneliness and a loss of purpose in their final years. It is a tragedy for the young. By exiling our elders, we have deprived our children of one of the most important relationships in their lives. We have cut them off from the stories, the wisdom, and the unconditional love of their grandparents. We have created a generation that has no meaningful contact with the bookends of the human lifespan, a generation that has little understanding of where it came from and where it is going. The loss of respect for elders is not just a moral failing; it is a profound act of self-harm.

The Tyranny of the Present

Our dishonouring of the past is not limited to our treatment of the elderly. It is evident in our entire cultural posture. We live in a state of perpetual presentism, a belief that only the 'now' matters. We have become obsessed with the new, the novel, the disruptive. We tear down statues, we rename buildings, we rewrite history books, not out of a genuine desire to learn from the past, but out of a narcissistic need to judge it by the standards of our own fleeting moment. We have forgotten that the past is not a collection of heroes and villains to be celebrated or condemned, but a complex tapestry of human beings, as flawed and as noble as we are, from whom we have much to learn.

This historical amnesia leaves us culturally and politically unmoored. We are easily swayed by simplistic ideologies and utopian promises, because we have no memory of where such ideas have led in the past. We are prone to panic and despair in the face of crisis, because we have no sense of the resilience and creativity that previous generations have shown in the face of their own challenges. A society without memory is a society without immunity. It is vulnerable to every passing political and cultural virus. To honour our father and mother is to honour the entire chain of being of which they are a part. It is to see ourselves not as the culmination of history, but as a single link in a long and venerable chain, with a duty to both those who came before us and those who will come after.

The Atomised Self

Underlying both the exile of the elders and the tyranny of the present is a deeper and more corrosive cultural force: **radical individualism**. As the writer Willow Liana has observed, we have become an **atomised** society. We have broken down the larger units of family, community, and tradition into their smallest component parts: the sovereign, autonomous individual. We have come to see freedom not as the ability to live a virtuous life within a web of mutual obligation, but as the right to be free from all constraints, from all unchosen bonds, from all duties that we have not explicitly consented to.

This vision of freedom is a mirage. It promises liberation, but it delivers loneliness. It tells us that we can be anything we want to be, that we can invent our own identity, that we are the sole authors of our own lives. But it leaves us utterly alone, disconnected from the very relationships that give life meaning and purpose. We have become a generation of lonely people, feeling, as one young woman put it, that "there are supposed to be people around, but they are missing."

The family is the primary casualty of this radical individualism. The bonds between parents and children, which were once seen as sacred and indissoluble, are now often viewed as temporary and conditional. We are told that we do not choose our parents, and therefore we have no obligation to them. We are encouraged to "find our own tribe," to surround ourselves with people who affirm our choices and validate our identities. But these chosen "tribes" are often fragile and fleeting, based on shared interests or lifestyles rather than on the deep, unconditional, and often difficult bonds of kinship. The Fifth Commandment is a direct repudiation of this atomised vision of the self. It reminds us that we are not self-created. We are born into a family, a history, a tradition. We are debtors, and our first debt is to those who gave us life. To honour them is to acknowledge this fundamental truth of our existence- even if, and maybe especially if– it requires sacrifice: doing it even if it is difficult and not doing it feels justified.

The Difficult Question: What If Our Parents Failed?

The Fifth Commandment presents a challenge that many find deeply uncomfortable. What if our parents were not honourable? What if they were abusive, neglectful, or absent? What if the secure base was never provided, and the internal working models we developed are ones of fear, mistrust, and unworthiness? Are we still commanded to honour them?

This is not a hypothetical question. The research on attachment makes clear that a significant minority of children grow up with insecure attachments. Some experience outright abuse or neglect. For these individuals, the command to "honour your father and your mother" can feel like a cruel joke, a demand to venerate the very people who caused them profound harm. How can we reconcile the commandment with this reality?

The answer lies in understanding what "honour" means. The Hebrew word *kavod*, translated as "honour," literally means "weight" or "gravity." To honour someone is to give them weight, to treat them as significant, to acknowledge their role in your life. It does not mean to approve of everything they did, to excuse their failures, or to pretend that harm did not occur. It requires a recognition of the reality of the relationship and a refusal to allow bitterness and resentment to define your life.

Consider the case of a man I will call David. David grew up with an alcoholic father who was verbally abusive and emotionally distant. His childhood was marked by fear, unpredictability, and a profound sense of unworthiness. As an adult, David struggled with relationships, with trust, with a persistent sense that he was fundamentally unlovable. For years, he was consumed by anger toward his father, an anger that coloured every aspect of his life. He cut off all contact, and he told himself that he had moved on. But he had not. His father still controlled him, not through presence, but through absence. The bitterness had become a prison.

It was only when David began to understand his father's own story—that his father had also grown up in an abusive home, that he had never learned how to be a father, that he was himself a broken man—that David began to find a path forward. He did not excuse his father's behaviour. He did not pretend that the harm had not occurred. But he began to see his father as a human being, flawed and tragic, rather than as a monster. He began to give his father "weight," to acknowledge the reality of their relationship without being defined by it. This was not easy. It required years of therapy, of grieving, of learning to separate his father's failures from his own worth. But in the end, it set him free. He was able to honour his father not because his father deserved it, but because David deserved to be free from the prison of bitterness.

This is the deeper wisdom of the Fifth Commandment. To honour our parents is not primarily about them; it is about us. It is about refusing to allow the failures of the past to define our future. It is about breaking the cycle of brokenness and choosing to be the secure base for the next generation that we perhaps never had ourselves. The commandment is not a denial of harm; it is a path through it.

The Chain That Binds Us: The Intergenerational Transmission

In 1990, the psychologist Mary Main, along with her colleague Judith Solomon, published a landmark paper that introduced a new and unsettling category of infant attachment: "disorganised." These were infants who didn't fit any of Ainsworth's original patterns. When their mothers returned after a brief separation, these babies would freeze, or rock back and forth, or display other bizarre and contradictory behaviours. They seemed to be caught in an impossible dilemma: their source of safety was also their source of fear.

Main and her other colleague, Erik Hesse, went on to discover the source of this disorganisation. It was almost always linked to unresolved trauma or loss in the parent's own life. A parent who had not come to terms with their own history of abuse, for example, would often engage in frightening or frightened behaviour toward their own child, without even realising it. The parent's past was literally being transmitted to the child in the present, creating a legacy of fear and confusion.

But Main also discovered something remarkable. Through the Adult Attachment Interview, which she developed with

Carol George and Nancy Kaplan, she found that she could predict, with startling accuracy, the attachment style of an infant based solely on an interview with the mother—before the child was even born. The key was not what had happened to the mother in her childhood, but how she had made sense of it. A mother who could reflect on her own attachment history, who could integrate the good and the bad into a coherent narrative, was overwhelmingly likely to have a securely attached child, regardless of her own difficult experiences. The cycle of trauma could be broken by the power of a redemptive story.

This finding encapsulates the profound truth of the Fifth Commandment. The way we relate to our own parents—the way we make sense of our own history, the way we honour or dishonour the intergenerational bond—shapes not just our own lives, but the lives of our children and our children's children. We are not isolated individuals. We are links in a chain that stretches back into the past and forward into the future. What we do with our link matters.

The Promise: A Long Life in the Land

The Fifth Commandment is unique among the Ten Commandments in that it comes with a promise: "that your days may be long in the land that the LORD your God is giving you." This is not a magical guarantee of individual longevity. It is a statement about the conditions for social and cultural survival. A society that honours the bond between generations is a society that will endure. A society that severs this bond will not.

The "land" is not just a geographical territory. It is a place of belonging, of stability, of cultural continuity. It is a place where the past is remembered, the present is meaningful, and the future is hopeful. To have a "long life in the land" is to be part of a story that is larger than ourselves, a story that began before we were born and will continue after we are gone. It is to live in a society that is stable, resilient, and capable of weathering the storms of history.

The aboriginal communities of Australia are some of the longest surviving societies - in no small part due to the reverence by which it treats their 'elders'. Even the deceased elders are not merely 'remembered' they are revered. In modern Australia, this trait is being exploited as performative 'theatre', and sadly will have the unintended consequence of eroding that reverence.

This is the promise of the Fifth Commandment. It is a promise of social cohesion, of cultural memory, of psychological health. And it is a promise that we are in grave danger of forfeiting. We have created a society that is adrift, a society that has forgotten its past and is therefore unable to navigate its future. We have created a generation of lonely, atomised individuals, disconnected from the very bonds that give life meaning and purpose.

But the law of honour is not a counsel of despair. It is a call to remembrance and to restoration. It is a call to turn back to our elders, to listen to their stories, to value their wisdom. It is a call to reclaim our history, to see it not as a source of shame, but as a source of strength. It is a call to rebuild the bonds of family and community, to recognise that our lives are not our own, but are woven into a web of mutual obligation and love. It is a call to honour our father and our mother, not just for their sake, but for our own, and for the sake of the generations to come. For in the end, a society that does not honour its past has no future.

At the deepest level, the Fifth Commandment is grounded in the Christian understanding of what it means to be human. We are not isolated, autonomous individuals. We are created in the image of a God who is himself relational—Father, Son, and Holy Spirit, eternally united in love. We are created for relationship, for community, for belonging. The bond between parent and child is the first and most fundamental of these relationships, the one that shapes all others.

When we honour our father and mother, we are participating in the very structure of reality. We are acknowledging that we are not self-made, that we are part of a story that is larger than ourselves, that we are embedded in a web of relationships that reflect the relational nature of God himself. This is why the commandment comes with a promise. A society that honours the intergenerational bond is a society that is aligned with the grain of the universe. It is a society that will flourish, that will have "a long life in the land."

Conversely, a society that severs this bond is a society that is working against the grain of reality. It is a society that will fragment, that will lose its way, that will ultimately collapse under the weight of its own loneliness and confusion. The modern West is discovering this truth the hard way. We have tried to build a society on the foundation of radical individualism, and we are reaping the consequences: epidemic loneliness, cultural amnesia, social fragmentation, and a profound loss of meaning and purpose.

The Fifth Commandment is an invitation to return. It is an invitation to remember who we are, where we come from, and where we are going. It is an invitation to rebuild the bonds that give life meaning and stability. It is an invitation to honour our father and our mother, not just for their sake, but for our own, and for the sake of all the generations to come.

The Restoration of Honour: Practical Steps

How, then, do we live out the law of honour in a society that has largely abandoned it? How do we rebuild the intergenerational bonds that have been so profoundly severed? There is no simple answer, but there are concrete steps we can take, both individually and collectively.

First, we must reconnect with our elders. This means more than the occasional phone call or holiday visit. It means making space in our lives for regular, meaningful contact with our parents and grandparents. It means asking them about their lives, their stories, their wisdom. It means allowing our children to develop real relationships with their grandparents, relationships that are not mediated by screens or limited to special occasions. For those whose parents or grandparents are no longer living, it means seeking out other elders in the community, recognising that the wisdom of age is not limited to our biological family.

Second, we must reclaim our history. This means resisting the tyranny of the present, the narcissistic belief that only our moment matters. It means reading the great books, studying the great events, understanding the ideas and movements that have shaped our world. It means teaching our children not just the facts of history, but the stories, the struggles, the triumphs and tragedies of those who came before us. It means seeing history not as a source of shame or pride, but as a source of wisdom, a vast repository of human experience from which we have much to learn.

Third, we must resist radical individualism. This means recognising that we are not self-created, that we are embedded in a web of relationships and obligations that we did not choose but which are nonetheless real and binding. It means valuing the bonds of family and community over the pursuit of individual autonomy. It means making sacrifices for the sake of our children, our parents, our communities. It means recognising that freedom is not the absence of constraints, but the ability to live a meaningful life within a web of mutual obligation and love.

Fourth, we must address the structural forces that undermine intergenerational bonds. This means rethinking our economic system, which often requires both parents to work full-time just to make ends meet, leaving little time or energy for the care of children or elderly parents. It means rethinking our housing patterns, which often scatter families across vast distances, making regular contact difficult or impossible. It means rethinking our care systems, finding ways to keep the elderly integrated into family and community life rather than exiling them to institutions. These are not easy problems, and they will require collective action and political will. But they are not insurmountable.

Finally, we must model honour for the next generation. Our children are watching. They are learning from us what it means to be a son or daughter, what it means to be a parent, what it means to be part of a family. If we honour our parents, if we value our elders, if we stay connected to our history, they will learn to do the same. If we do not, they will not. The intergenerational transmission of honour, like the intergenerational transmission of attachment, is not automatic. It must be taught, modelled, and lived.

The Test: Are We Honouring the Intergenerational Bond?

As with the previous commandments, it is worth asking ourselves some diagnostic questions to assess whether we are truly living out the law of honour. These questions are not meant to induce guilt, but to provoke honest self-reflection.

Do we make time for our parents and grandparents? Not just obligatory visits, but genuine, unhurried time where we listen to their stories, seek their counsel, and allow them to be part of our lives. Or have we relegated them to the margins, seeing them as burdens to be managed rather than treasures to be valued?

Do we allow our children to develop real relationships with their grandparents? Or have we, through distance or busyness or conflict, deprived them of this vital connection? Are our children growing up with a sense of where they come from, or are they rootless, disconnected from the generations that preceded them?

Do we know our family history? Can we tell our children the stories of their great-grandparents, the struggles they faced, the values they held, the sacrifices they made? Or have we allowed these stories to be lost, severing our connection to the past?

How do we speak about our parents? Do we speak of them with respect and gratitude, even when acknowledging their failures? Or do we speak of them with contempt, bitterness, or dismissal? Our words shape not only our own hearts, but the hearts of our children, who are learning from us what it means to honour.

Are we taking responsibility for the intergenerational transmission of wisdom and values? Are we consciously passing on to our children the best of what we have received, while working to break the cycles of dysfunction? Or are we simply reacting, allowing the patterns of the past to repeat themselves unconsciously?

How do we treat the elderly in general? Do we see them as valuable members of our community, with wisdom and experience to offer? Or do we see them as irrelevant, as obstacles to progress, as people whose time has passed? Our treatment of the elderly in general reveals our true attitude toward the intergenerational bond.

These questions are searching, and the answers may be uncomfortable. But they are necessary. The Fifth Commandment is not a vague sentiment about being nice to our parents. It is a fundamental principle about the structure of a healthy society. A society that honours the intergenerational bond is a society that can endure. A society that severs this bond is a society that is, quite literally, dying.

Conclusion: The Chain That Cannot Be Broken

The modern world has tried to break the chain that binds generation to generation. It has told us that we are self-made, that we owe nothing to the past, that we can invent ourselves anew in every generation. But this is a lie, and it is a lie that is destroying us. We are not self-made. We are the product of countless generations, of countless acts of love and sacrifice and wisdom. We are debtors, and our first debt is to those who gave us life.

To honour our father and mother is to acknowledge this debt. It is to recognise that we are part of a story that is larger than ourselves. It is to take responsibility for our link in the chain, to pass on the best of what we have received, and to break the cycles of brokenness that we have inherited. It is to ensure that the generations to come will have a secure base from which to explore the world, a rich inheritance of wisdom and values, and a sense of belonging to something greater than themselves.

This is the promise of the Fifth Commandment: that if we honour the intergenerational bond, our days will be long in the land. Not because God will magically extend our individual lifespans, but because a society that honours its past has a future. A society that severs itself from its roots will wither and die. But a society that remembers, that honours, that passes on the great inheritance of human wisdom from generation to generation—that society will endure.

The choice is ours. Will we honour our father and our mother? Will we rebuild the bonds that have been severed? Will we take our place in the great chain of being, recognising that we are neither the beginning nor the end, but a vital link between past and future? The answer to these questions will determine not just our own flourishing, but the flourishing of all the generations to come.

Chapter 6: Lex Vitae - The Law of Life

> *You shall not murder. (Exodus 20:13)*

In the rolling green hills of Rwanda, in a small village where the scent of eucalyptus hung in the air, lived a farmer named Jean-Pierre. He was, by all accounts, an ordinary man. His hands were calloused from a lifetime of working the rich, red earth. His laughter was loud, especially after a few Primus beers at the local bar. He was a husband to a wife he adored, a father to three children who were his pride, a neighbour who could be counted on to help with a harvest or lend a tool. He was Hutu, but this was a simple fact of his existence, like the colour of his eyes or the shape of his hands. His best friend and neighbour, a man named Michel, was Tutsi. They had grown up together, their childhoods a tangle of shared secrets and scraped knees. Their children played hide-and-seek among the banana trees that separated their homes. Their wives, inseparable, traded recipes and gossip over the fence. Their lives were woven together in the thousand small, sturdy threads of true community.

Then, in April 1994, the threads began to unravel. The president's plane, a silver bird in the African sky, was shot down, and a madness, carefully cultivated for years, was unleashed. The radio, once a source of music and news, became a serpent, whispering poison into the airwaves. The voices on Radio Télévision Libre des Mille Collines (RTLM) were slick, charismatic, and utterly terrifying. They spoke of the Tutsi not as neighbours, not as friends, not as fellow Rwandans, but as "inyenzi," cockroaches. The word, repeated relentlessly, began to crawl under the skin of the nation. Cockroaches, the voices explained, were not human. They were invaders, pests, a filth that had to be cleansed. To kill a Tutsi, the radio hosts laughed, was not a crime. It was a patriotic duty, a public health measure.

At first, Jean-Pierre scoffed. This was the talk of extremists in the capital, Kigali. It had nothing to do with his life, with his village, with Michel. But the poison spread. The local mayor, a man Jean-Pierre had respected, held a meeting in the village square. His words were a chilling echo of the radio's hate. He spoke of a final war, of the need to protect their Hutu identity. Soldiers, their faces grim and impassive, arrived in trucks, distributing crates of new, sharp machetes. Neighbours who had once shared beers were now organised into "Interahamwe," the killing squads. To refuse to join was to become a suspect, an "ibyitso," a traitor, complicit with the cockroaches. To refuse was to risk having your own name added to a list.

One night, the Interahamwe came to Jean-Pierre's door. They were not strangers; they were the men he had known his whole life. But their eyes were different, glazed with a mixture of cheap beer and ideological fervour. They were chanting the songs from the radio. They had a list. Michel's name was on it. One of them, a man who had been the best man at Jean-Pierre's wedding, handed him a machete. "It is your turn," he said, his voice slurring. "Prove you are with us. Prove you are a true Hutu."

In that moment, standing in the flickering lamplight of his own home, with the sounds of his sleeping children in the next room, something inside Jean-Pierre broke. The intricate wiring of a lifetime of friendship, of shared humanity, short-circuited. The man who had shared his wedding day with Michel, the man whose children played with Michel's children, the man who had called Michel his brother, took the machete. The cold weight of it in his hand was a terrible, final reality. He walked across the small patch of land that separated their homes, a distance he had crossed a thousand times in peace. And he did the unthinkable.

How does an ordinary man, a man who is not a monster, become a murderer? How does a community of neighbours become a field of slaughter? The story of Jean-Pierre, and the story of the Rwandan genocide, is not a story about a nation of psychopaths. It is a story about the terrifying fragility of human morality, about the psychological mechanisms that allow ordinary people to commit extraordinary evil. And it is a story that reveals the profound, life-or-death importance of the Sixth Commandment: "You shall not murder." This is not just a prohibition against unlawful killing. It is a firewall against the darkest potential of the human heart. It is a declaration that every human life is sacred, inviolable, and possessed of a dignity that no government, no ideology, and no mob can ever extinguish.

The Empathy Circuit: The Brain's Built-in Firewall

To understand how the firewall of the Sixth Commandment can be breached, we must first understand how it is built. We are not, as a species, naturally inclined to kill one another. In fact, our brains are wired with a powerful set of mechanisms designed to prevent us from doing so. At the heart of this system is **empathy**, the ability to understand and share the feelings of another.

In the 1990s, a team of Italian neuroscientists led by Giacomo Rizzolatti made a remarkable discovery. While studying the brains of macaque monkeys, they found a special class of neurons that fired not only when the monkey performed an action, but also when it observed another monkey performing the same action. They called these **mirror neurons**. It was as if the monkey's brain was simulating the other's experience, creating a shared neural reality. Later research confirmed that humans have a similar, and even more sophisticated, mirror neuron system.

This system is the foundation of our ability to empathize. As neuroscientist Marco Iacoboni and his colleagues have shown, when we see someone expressing an emotion—a smile of joy, a grimace of pain—our mirror neurons fire, activating the same emotional circuits in our own brains. We don't just cognitively understand their emotion; we feel it, in a diluted form, in ourselves. This is what researchers like Tania Singer and Hedy Engen call the **affective** component of empathy: "I feel what you feel."

This shared emotional experience is processed in a network of brain regions often called the "empathy circuit." Key nodes in this circuit include the **anterior insula**, a region deep within the brain that is crucial for interoception, our sense of our own bodily states. When we feel our own pain, the anterior insula lights up. When we see someone else in pain, it lights up again. It is, in a very real sense, the seat of our ability to feel another's suffering. The **anterior cingulate cortex (ACC)** is involved in processing the emotional distress associated with pain. Like the insula, the ACC is active both when we are in pain and when we witness the pain of others. The **inferior frontal cortex** (including the pars opercularis, where mirror neurons are abundant) and the **inferior parietal lobule** are involved in understanding the actions and intentions of others.

Together, these regions create a powerful, automatic, and deeply ingrained system for connecting with other people. This system is our first line of defence against violence. It is hard to harm someone when you are literally feeling their pain. The Sixth Commandment, then, is not an arbitrary rule imposed from the outside. It is a moral articulation of a deep neurological reality. It is a command to listen to the wisdom of our own brains, to honour the built-in firewall that makes compassion possible and violence difficult.

The Dehumanization Switch: Turning Off Empathy

If our brains are wired for empathy, how is it possible for a man like Jean-Pierre to murder his neighbour? How are atrocities like the Rwandan genocide possible? The answer is as simple as it is terrifying: the empathy circuit can be turned off. And the switch that turns it off is **dehumanization**.

Dehumanization is the psychological process of viewing another person or group as less than human. It is a cognitive loophole that allows us to bypass the moral and emotional constraints that normally govern our interactions with others. As the social psychologist Susan Fiske and the neuroscientist Lasana Harris have shown, when we dehumanize someone, we literally stop seeing them as a person. Our brains stop processing them as a fellow human being with a mind, with feelings, with a life of their own.

In a series of groundbreaking fMRI studies, Harris and Fiske showed participants images of people from different social groups. When participants viewed images of people they respected (like Olympic athletes) or pitied (like the elderly), the social cognition network in their brains—including the medial prefrontal cortex (MPFC), which is crucial for thinking about the minds of others—lit up as expected. But when they viewed images of people from dehumanized groups, like homeless people or drug addicts, this network remained eerily silent. It was as if the participants' brains were not even registering them as human. Instead, the brain region that lit up was the **anterior insula**, the same region associated with disgust toward spoiled food or foul odours.

This is the neural signature of dehumanization. The brain literally shifts from a "person" processing network to an "object" or "animal" processing network. The dehumanized other is no longer a "who," but a "what." And once someone is a "what," the rules of morality no longer apply. You don't feel empathy for a cockroach. You don't feel compassion for a vermin. You exterminate it.

This is precisely what happened in Rwanda. The constant barrage of propaganda describing the Tutsi as "inyenzi" was not just political rhetoric. It was a systematic campaign of psychological warfare designed to flip the dehumanization switch in the brains of the Hutu population. By relentlessly associating the Tutsi with a disgusting and disease-carrying insect, the propaganda hijacked the brain's disgust circuitry, overriding the natural empathy that Hutu like Jean-Pierre would have felt for their Tutsi neighbours. The radio told them that Michel was not a person; he was a cockroach. And when the killing squad came to his door, Jean-Pierre's brain, tragically, believed it.

The Eight Doors of Moral Disengagement

Dehumanization is the most powerful tool for enabling violence, but it is not the only one. The psychologist Albert

Bandura, in his seminal work on moral agency, identified eight distinct mechanisms of **moral disengagement**—the psychological manoeuvres we use to selectively switch off our moral self-sanctions and do things we would normally consider wrong. These mechanisms are the eight doors through which ordinary people can walk to commit atrocities.

First, **moral justification** reframes harmful conduct as serving a higher moral purpose. "I am not murdering; I am cleansing the nation." Second, **euphemistic labelling** uses sanitized, convoluted language to make harmful actions seem respectable. "I am not killing people; I am engaging in 'ethnic cleansing.'" Third, **advantageous comparison** compares one's actions to even worse atrocities to make them seem trivial or even righteous. "What we are doing is nothing compared to what they did to us." Fourth, **displacement of responsibility** sees oneself as merely an instrument of a higher authority. "I was just following orders." Fifth, **diffusion of responsibility** spreads the responsibility for an action across a group, so that no single individual feels personally accountable. "Everyone was doing it." Sixth, **disregarding or distorting the consequences** minimizes, ignores, or misconstrues the harm caused by one's actions. "They are not really suffering." Seventh, **dehumanization** strips people of their human qualities, as we have seen. Eighth, **attribution of blame** sees the victims as responsible for their own suffering. "They brought this on themselves."

These mechanisms were all at play in Rwanda. The killing was morally justified as a defence of the nation. Euphemistic language was used on the radio. The Hutu were told that their actions were nothing compared to the past oppression by the Tutsi. People displaced responsibility onto the authorities and diffused it among the mob. They were encouraged to ignore the suffering of their victims, who were dehumanized as cockroaches and blamed for their own fate.

These are not exotic, foreign mechanisms. We see them at work all around us, in more subtle but still insidious forms. We see them in the online world, where the anonymity and distance of the internet make it easy to dehumanize those with whom we disagree, to hurl insults and threats that we would never say to someone's face. A 2020 study by psychologists at Princeton found that online dehumanization is strongly correlated with support for political violence. People who described their political opponents using dehumanizing language (calling them "animals," "vermin," or "subhuman" or as Hillary Clinton did when she called Trump supporters "deplorables") were significantly more likely to endorse violent actions against them.

We see moral disengagement in our political discourse, where opponents are not just wrong, but evil, where complex issues are reduced to simplistic morality plays, and where moral justification is used to excuse all manner of incivility and even violence. We see them in the corporate world, where diffusion of responsibility allows for decisions that harm thousands, with no single person feeling accountable. The 2008 financial crisis is a case study in this. No single banker felt responsible for the collapse because everyone was "just doing their job," following the incentives of the system. The harm to millions of ordinary people was disregarded or distorted as an unfortunate but necessary consequence of market forces.

Bandura's work is a chilling reminder that the capacity for evil is not limited to a few monstrous individuals. It is a universal human potential, a dark door that can be unlocked by the right psychological keys. The Sixth Commandment is a lock on that door. It is a simple, absolute, and non-negotiable prohibition that cuts through all the self-serving justifications and rationalizations. It says: No. No matter how you frame it, no matter who orders it, no matter what they have done, you shall not murder. You shall not take a human life.

The Banality of Evil: The Desk-Bound Killer

When we think of evil, we often picture monsters. We imagine sadistic psychopaths, driven by a lust for cruelty. But one of the most disturbing lessons of the 20th century is that the greatest evils are often committed not by monsters, but by ordinary people. They are committed by bureaucrats filling out forms, by train dispatchers scheduling routes, by clerks managing supplies. They are committed by people who, in the words of the political theorist Hannah Arendt, are not monstrous, but "terrifyingly normal."

Arendt coined the phrase "the banality of evil" to describe what she observed at the trial of Adolf Eichmann, one of the chief architects of the Holocaust. She expected to find a diabolical mastermind, a twisted anti-Semitic fanatic. Instead, she found a bland, mediocre bureaucrat. Eichmann was not a foaming-at-the-mouth ideologue; he was a careerist, a joiner, a man whose primary motivation seemed to be a desire to do his job well. He spoke in clichés and stock phrases, a testament to his "inability to think." He was not a monster, Arendt concluded. He was a nobody. And that was the most terrifying thing of all.

Eichmann's evil was banal because it was thoughtless. He was not motivated by a deep-seated hatred of Jews, but by a desire to be an efficient administrator. He was a master of moral disengagement. He displaced responsibility to his superiors ("I was just following orders"). He used euphemistic language ("transportation," "final solution"). He disregarded the consequences of his actions, focusing only on the logistical challenge of moving millions of people to their deaths. He was, in his own mind, simply a cog in a machine, a man doing his job.

This is a profoundly unsettling idea. It suggests that the most dangerous people are not necessarily those who are filled with hate, but those who have stopped thinking. It is the person who has outsourced their conscience to an ideology, a corporation, or a state. It is the person who has become so absorbed in the means that they have lost sight of the ends. It is the person who has allowed their moral world to shrink to the size of their job description.

This is the subtle, modern form of violence that the Sixth Commandment also forbids. It is the murder of the soul that precedes the murder of the body. It is the choice to stop seeing the human being at the other end of the form, the other end of the supply chain, the other end of the drone strike. It is the choice to reduce a person to a number, a statistic, a problem to be managed. The commandment "You shall not murder" is not just a prohibition against pulling a trigger or wielding a machete. It is a command to think, to feel, to see the human face in front of us, and to never, ever allow ourselves to become cogs in a machine of death.

The Image of God: The Unshakeable Foundation of Human Worth

Why? Why is human life so sacred? Why is murder the ultimate transgression? The modern secular world struggles to answer this question. It may appeal to concepts like human rights, or social contracts, or the utilitarian calculus of maximising happiness. But all of these are ultimately fragile foundations. Rights can be revoked, contracts can be broken, and the happiness of the many can be used to justify the sacrifice of the few. None of these provide an absolute, unshakeable foundation for the inviolability of human life.

The Christian tradition provides a different answer, an answer that is both more profound and more resilient. Human life is sacred not because of what we can do, or what we have, or what the state says about us. Human life is sacred because we are created in the **imago Dei**, the image of God.

This is the radical declaration of the very first chapter of the Bible: "So God created man in his own image, in the image of God he created him; male and female he created them" (Genesis 1:27). This was a revolutionary idea in the ancient world, a world where the king or the pharaoh might be considered divine, but ordinary people were expendable. **The Bible declares that every single human being, regardless of race, or gender, or status, or ability, bears the indelible stamp of the Creator.** Every person is a living, breathing icon of God himself.

To murder a human being, therefore, is not just to end a biological life. It is to commit an act of sacrilege. It is to deface an icon, to shatter a reflection of God in the world. It is to usurp a prerogative that belongs to God alone, the author and giver of life. This is why the Sixth Commandment is so absolute. It is not a suggestion, or a guideline, or a piece of prudential advice. It is a recognition of a fundamental metaphysical reality. Human life is not our own to take.

This is a truth that our modern world has largely forgotten, and we are paying a terrible price. When we lose the sense of the *imago Dei*, we are left with a purely materialistic and utilitarian view of human beings. People are no longer ends in themselves, but means to an end. They are producers, or consumers, or voters, or obstacles. Their value is not inherent, but instrumental. And if they cease to be useful, or if they become inconvenient, they can be discarded.

This is the logic that leads, ultimately, to the gas chamber and the gulag. It is the logic that allows us to see the unborn child as a clump of cells, the elderly person with dementia as a burden on the healthcare system, the political opponent as an obstacle to progress. It is the logic of Jean-Pierre, who saw his neighbour not as an icon of God, but as a cockroach to be crushed. The Sixth Commandment is the great bulwark against this logic. It is a constant, unwavering reminder that every human life has an infinite, unquantifiable, and sacred worth.

The Test: Are We Living the Law of Life?

Most of us will never be in Jean-Pierre's position. We will never be handed a machete and told to kill our neighbour. But the spirit of the Sixth Commandment goes far beyond the physical act of murder. It is a call to honour and protect the sacredness of human life in all its forms. And if we are honest with ourselves, we can see the ways in which we violate this spirit every day.

Do we engage in dehumanising language, online or in person? Do we speak of our political opponents as monsters, or idiots, or enemies? Do we participate in the outrage mobs that seek to destroy the reputation and livelihood of those who have transgressed some social norm? Do we secretly delight in the downfall of others? This is the logic of dehumanization, the first step on the road to violence.

Do we treat people as means to an end? Do we see our employees as mere instruments of profit, our colleagues as rivals to be overcome, our romantic partners as sources of our own gratification? Do we value people for what they can do for us, rather than for who they are? This is the logic of utilitarianism, the denial of the *imago Dei*.

Do we turn a blind eye to the suffering of the vulnerable? Do we ignore the plight of the homeless, the refugee, the victim of injustice? Do we comfort ourselves with the thought that it is not our problem, that they brought it on themselves, that there is nothing we can do? This is the logic of moral disengagement, the abdication of our responsibility to protect the sacredness of life.

Do we harbour hatred, bitterness, or a desire for revenge in our hearts? Jesus, in the Sermon on the Mount, radicalizes the Sixth Commandment, tracing the act of murder back to its source in the human heart. "You have heard that it was said to those of old, 'You shall not murder; and whoever murders will be liable to judgment.' But I say to you that everyone who is angry with his brother will be liable to judgment." (Matthew 5:21-22). The physical act of murder is simply the fruit. The seed is the anger and contempt we hold in our hearts.

Conclusion: The Choice for Life

The Sixth Commandment is not a restriction on our freedom. It is the very condition of our freedom. A society that does not protect the sacredness of human life is a society that will inevitably descend into fear, violence, and tyranny. It is only when we know that our lives are safe, that we cannot be killed with impunity, that we can be truly free—free to speak, free to disagree, free to create, free to live.

The story of Jean-Pierre is a tragedy. It is the story of an ordinary man who was pushed, step by step, through the doors of moral disengagement until he committed an act that shattered his own soul and the soul of his nation. But the story of Rwanda is also a story of hope. It is a story of survivors who have chosen to forgive, of perpetrators who have confessed and repented, of a nation that is struggling, day by day, to rebuild the bonds of community and to reclaim the truth that every life is sacred.

And it is a story that contains a vital lesson for us all. The line between good and evil does not run between nations, or races, or political parties. It runs, as Aleksandr Solzhenitsyn wrote, right through the middle of every human heart. The capacity for violence and the capacity for compassion both lie within us. The Sixth Commandment is a call to choose. It is a call to starve the wolf of hatred and to feed the wolf of love. It is a call to turn off the switch of dehumanization and to turn on the circuit of empathy. It is a call to see in every human face not a cockroach, not an obstacle, not an enemy, but an icon of God, a sacred life, a brother or a sister.

It is a call to choose life, that we and our children may live.

The Neuroscience of Violence: When the Firewall Fails

Understanding how ordinary people become capable of murder requires us to look more deeply at what happens in the brain when the empathy circuit fails. Recent neuroscience research has revealed that the capacity for violence is not simply the absence of empathy, but an active process involving multiple brain systems working in concert.

When we dehumanize someone, the medial prefrontal cortex (MPFC)—the region responsible for thinking about the minds of others—shows reduced activity. But simultaneously, other brain regions become more active. The amygdala, our brain's threat detection system, can become hyperactive when we perceive someone as an enemy or a danger. This creates a perfect storm: we stop seeing the other person as human (reduced MPFC activity) while simultaneously perceiving them as a threat (increased amygdala activity). The result is that violence becomes not just possible, but psychologically justified.

Research by neuroscientist James Fallon has shown that even individuals with psychopathic brain patterns (reduced activity in empathy circuits) do not inevitably become violent. What matters is the environment, the social context, and crucially, the moral framework within which a person operates. This is why the Sixth Commandment is so vital. It provides an external moral anchor that can hold even when our internal emotional circuits are compromised by fear, ideology, or social pressure.

The Rwandan genocide provides a tragic natural experiment in this regard. Sociologist Hollie Nyseth Brehm's analysis of over one million court cases revealed that perpetrators were not randomly distributed across the population. They clustered in families and social networks. If one brother participated in killing, his siblings were far more likely to do so as well. This suggests that violence is not just an individual psychological phenomenon, but a social contagion that spreads through networks of trust and obligation.

But here is the crucial finding: even in the communes with the highest levels of violence, only about 20 percent of Hutu men participated in killing. Four out of five did not. This means that even under extreme social pressure, even when surrounded by dehumanizing propaganda, even when their friends and family members were participating, the majority of people refused to cross the line. Something in them held. Perhaps it was a stronger empathy circuit. Perhaps it was a different social network. Perhaps it was a deeper moral conviction. But whatever it was, it was enough.

This is the hope embedded in the Sixth Commandment. It is not a naive hope that humans are naturally good, or that we will never be tempted to violence. It is a realistic hope that recognizes our capacity for evil, but also our capacity for moral resistance. It is a hope that says: even in the darkest circumstances, even when the empathy circuit is under assault, even when everyone around you is participating in atrocity, you can choose differently. You can refuse. You can hold the line.

The Path Forward: Rebuilding the Firewall

If dehumanization is the mechanism by which the empathy circuit is switched off, then **re-humanisation** is the mechanism by which it can be switched back on. And this is not just a theoretical possibility. It is something that has been demonstrated, again and again, in the aftermath of atrocities.

In Rwanda, one of the most remarkable aspects of the post-genocide recovery has been the "Gacaca" courts, a traditional form of community justice adapted for the massive scale of the genocide. In these courts, perpetrators and survivors sat together in the same space. Perpetrators were required to confess their crimes in detail, to name their victims, to describe what they had done. And survivors were given the opportunity to speak, to tell their stories, to confront those who had harmed them.

This was not an easy process. It was painful, traumatic, and often re-traumatizing. But it was also profoundly humanizing. When Jean-Pierre (or men like him) stood in front of the community and confessed, "I killed Michel. I took his life with my own hands," he was forced to see Michel not as a cockroach, but as a person. A person with a name. A person with a family. A person whose absence left a hole in the community. And when Michel's widow stood and spoke of her husband, of the man he had been, of the life they had shared, she was forcing everyone present to see Michel's humanity.

This is the power of testimony, of truth-telling, of bearing witness. It is the power to re-humanise. And it is a power that we all possess. Every time we choose to see the person behind the label, the human being behind the statistic, the face behind the screen name, we are engaging in an act of re-humanization. Every time we choose to listen to someone's story, to acknowledge their pain, to recognize their dignity, we are rebuilding the empathy circuit, both in ourselves and in our communities.

The Sixth Commandment, then, is not just a prohibition. It is also an invitation. It is an invitation to see every human being as an icon of God, to treat every life as sacred, to build a world in which violence is not just illegal, but unthinkable. It is an invitation to choose life, in all its fullness, in all its complexity, in all its sacred, irreducible dignity.

Chapter 7: Lex Fidelitatis - The Law of Fidelity

You shall not commit adultery. (Exodus 20:14)

In July 2015, a group of hackers calling themselves "The Impact Team" breached the servers of Avid Life Media, the parent company of a website whose very existence was a monument to broken promises: Ashley Madison. The site's slogan, a cynical jingle of infidelity, was "Life is short. Have an affair." For years, it had operated in the shadowy corners of the internet, a digital speakeasy for those looking to cheat on their partners. It promised its users absolute discretion, a secret world where they could indulge their desires without consequence. It was a lie built on top of a million other lies.

The Impact Team announced their hack not with a quiet ransom note, but with a public ultimatum. They declared Ashley Madison a fraudulent, immoral enterprise, and demanded that Avid Life Media shut it down permanently. If the company refused, the hackers would release the personal information of all 37 million users: names, email addresses, credit card details, and sexual fantasies. The company refused. And The Impact Team kept their promise.

What followed was a digital apocalypse. A data file nearly 10 gigabytes in size was uploaded to the dark web, and within hours, it had been downloaded, dissected, and made searchable. The secrets were out. The consequences were immediate and devastating. Marriages imploded. Careers were ruined. Public figures were disgraced. At least two suicides were linked to the leak. The data revealed a geography of betrayal, with postcodes in affluent suburbs lighting up as hotspots of infidelity. It exposed the mundane reality behind the fantasy: the site was overwhelmingly male, with thousands of the female profiles reportedly being fake, created by the company to lure in paying customers. The whole enterprise, it seemed, was a con from top to bottom.

One of the names in that data dump belonged to John, a pastor from a small town in the American South. He was a respected community leader, a man known for his stirring sermons on the importance of family and faith. He had a wife he had known since high school and two teenage children. To the outside world, his life was a model of Christian virtue. But inside, John was living a lie. For years, he had been struggling with a secret addiction to pornography, which had escalated into online affairs. Ashley Madison was his digital sanctuary, a place where he could be a different person, a person without vows, without responsibilities, without a conscience.

When the news of the hack broke, John was plunged into a state of panic. He prayed it would all blow over, that his name would be lost in the sea of data. But it wasn't. A local journalist, running the names of prominent community members through a search tool, found him. The story ran on the front page of the local paper. The secret was out. His life, as he knew it, was over. His wife, devastated, filed for divorce. His children, confused and angry, refused to speak to him. His church, feeling betrayed, asked for his resignation. John lost everything: his family, his job, his home, his reputation. He was a man adrift, a ghost in his own life, haunted by the wreckage of his broken promises.

The Ashley Madison hack was more than just a celebrity scandal or a tech story. It was a stark, brutal lesson in the importance of the Seventh Commandment. It revealed, on a massive scale, what happens when the bonds of fidelity are broken. The pain, the chaos, the destruction—it was not just emotional. It was a systemic collapse of trust that radiated outwards, shattering families, communities, and the lives of millions. The story of John, and the thousands like him, is the story of what happens when we forget that our promises are not just words, but the very architecture of our social world. It is a story that forces us to ask: why does fidelity matter so much? And what, exactly, is happening in our brains and in our societies when we break it?

The Chemistry of Commitment: The Brain in Love

To understand the devastation of betrayal, we must first understand the miracle of the bond. The intense, focused, and often irrational connection we feel for a romantic partner is not a mere cultural script or a poetic fancy. It is a profound neurobiological event, a sophisticated cocktail of ancient chemicals that wires two individuals together. And the key ingredients in this cocktail are two tiny neuropeptides: **oxytocin** and **vasopressin**.

For decades, scientists studied these chemicals in a small, unassuming rodent: the prairie vole. Unlike most mammals, prairie voles are famously monogamous. After a period of intense mating, a male and female will form a lifelong pair-bond, nesting together, raising their young together, and aggressively rejecting any other potential mates. Their promiscuous cousins, the montane voles, do no such thing. They mate and move on. The difference, scientists discovered, lies in the brain's response to oxytocin and vasopressin.

In monogamous prairie voles, the brain's reward centres—particularly the nucleus accumbens—are densely packed with receptors for oxytocin and vasopressin. When they mate, a flood of these chemicals is released, binding to these receptors and linking the pleasure of the reward system to the specific scent and sight of their partner. As neuroscientist Larry Young and his colleagues have shown, the partner's identity becomes stamped into the brain's circuitry. They are no longer just *a* vole; they are *the* vole. The bond is so powerful that if you inject a female prairie vole with oxytocin, she will form a pair-bond with the nearest male, even without mating. Conversely, if you block the oxytocin receptors, she will mate but never form a bond.

Humans, of course, are not prairie voles. But we have the same basic neurochemical toolkit. Oxytocin, often called the "cuddle hormone," is released during moments of social bonding: between a mother and her infant, between friends sharing a meal, and, most powerfully, during sexual intimacy between romantic partners. It reduces anxiety, increases feelings of trust, and promotes a sense of calm and connection. Vasopressin, its chemical cousin, plays a crucial role in mate-guarding and protective behaviours. It is the neurochemical root of the feeling that says, "This person is mine to protect."

When we fall in love and form a committed relationship, our brains are doing something remarkable. They are harnessing this ancient bonding system and focusing it, with laser-like intensity, on one person. The touch, the scent, the voice of our partner become associated with a flood of oxytocin, creating a powerful feedback loop of attachment and reward. This is why being with our partner feels like coming home. It is why, in the early stages of love, we can feel almost addicted to their presence. Our brain has been rewired to see them as essential to our well-being.

The Seventh Commandment, then, is not an arbitrary rule against a particular kind of fun. It is a recognition of the profound biological and psychological reality of the pair-bond. It is a command to honour the sacred neurochemistry of commitment, to protect the delicate wiring that binds two people together. Adultery is not just a breach of a social contract. It is a direct assault on this neural architecture. It introduces a foreign signal into a closed system, a rival scent into the nest. It is an act of neurological vandalism.

The Agony of the Break: The Body Keeps the Score

If the formation of a pair-bond is a neurochemical miracle, its dissolution is a neurochemical catastrophe. The pain of betrayal is not, as some might suggest, "all in your head." It is a real, measurable, physiological event. Your body experiences infidelity as a profound threat to its survival, and it reacts accordingly.

As we saw in the research by Blumenthal and Young, the loss of a partner—whether through death or betrayal—activates the same regions of the brain that process physical pain. The anterior cingulate cortex and the insula, the brain's primary pain centres, light up. This is why betrayal can literally feel like a punch to the gut or a knife in the heart. Your brain is not distinguishing between physical and emotional pain; to the brain, pain is pain.

But it goes deeper. The sudden withdrawal of the constant, low-level supply of oxytocin that comes from a stable partnership throws the brain's stress-response system into overdrive. The body is flooded with stress hormones like cortisol and adrenaline. The heart races, blood pressure rises, and the immune system is suppressed. Research has shown that in the immediate aftermath of a partner's death, the surviving partner has a significantly elevated risk of heart attack and stroke. The same physiological crisis occurs in the aftermath of betrayal. The body is in a state of emergency.

This is the biological reality behind the emotional turmoil of infidelity. The anxiety, the depression, the obsessive thoughts, the inability to eat or sleep—these are not signs of weakness. They are the predictable symptoms of a brain and body in crisis. The secure base of attachment has been ripped away, and the world no longer feels safe. The person who was the primary source of comfort has become the primary source of threat. This is a profound psychological paradox, and it can lead to a form of trauma known as Post-Traumatic Stress Disorder (PTSD). The flashbacks, the nightmares, the hypervigilance—these are the hallmarks of a mind that has been deeply wounded.

The commandment against adultery is a recognition of this devastating potential. It is a law designed to protect us from the profound, soul-shattering pain of betrayal. It is a guardrail against the kind of psychological and physiological damage that can take years, or even a lifetime, to heal.

The Cognitive Cost of Deceit: The Burden of the Lie

While the betrayed partner is plunged into a world of pain, the unfaithful partner enters a different kind of hell: the prison of the lie. As we explored in the previous chapter, lying is hard work. It is a cognitively demanding task that consumes a vast amount of mental energy.

As the research by Iris Blandón-Gitlin and her colleagues has shown, telling the truth is relatively easy. You simply have to access a memory and report it. But to tell a lie, you must engage in a complex series of mental operations. First, you must suppress the truth, which is often automatically activated in your mind. Second, you must invent a plausible alternative narrative. Third, you must constantly monitor this narrative for internal consistency and for consistency with any other known facts. Fourth, you must manage your own behaviour to appear truthful and to avoid leaking any signs of deception. This is a massive cognitive load, and it is exhausting.

Infidelity is not a single lie, but a whole system of lies. It is a second life that must be constructed and maintained in parallel with your real life. Every text message must be scrutinized, every email deleted, every credit card statement checked. You must keep your stories straight, your alibis consistent. You must manage the constant fear of exposure. This is not just a moral burden; it is a cognitive one. The mental resources that are being poured into maintaining the deception are resources that are not available for other things: for your work, for your children, for your own personal growth.

This is the reality behind what researchers Alisa Bedrov and Shelly Gable call the **secrecy burden**. Their work has shown that keeping a significant secret has a profound negative impact on well-being. It leads to lower authenticity, higher rates of depression and anxiety, and a pervasive sense of social isolation. The secret-keeper is living in a state of constant, low-level stress, always on guard, never fully able to relax. They are alienated not only from their partner, but from themselves. They are performing a role, and the strain of that performance is immense.

The commandment against adultery, then, is also an act of mercy for the potential adulterer. It is a warning against the corrosive, soul-destroying burden of the lie. It is a call to live in the freedom of the truth, to have a single, integrated self, to not be torn apart by the cognitive and emotional demands of a double life. Fidelity is not just a gift to your partner; it is a gift to yourself. It is the gift of a clear conscience and an undivided mind.

The Modern Assault on Fidelity: A Culture of Betrayal

If the costs of infidelity are so high, why is it so common? The answer is that we live in a culture that is actively hostile to the idea of lifelong fidelity. We are surrounded by messages and technologies that encourage us to see our relationships not as covenants to be kept, but as consumer products to be upgraded.

First, we have embraced a **consumer mindset** in our romantic lives. Dating apps have turned potential partners into a deck of cards to be swiped left or right. We are encouraged to shop for the perfect partner, to look for someone who will meet all of our needs, to keep our options open. This is the logic of the marketplace, not the logic of the covenant. A covenant says, "I am yours, for better or for worse." The market says, "I am yours, until a better offer comes along." This mindset creates a pervasive sense of provisionality in our relationships. We are never fully committed, because we are always secretly wondering if there is someone better out there.

Second, we are drowning in a sea of **exploitative systems**, most notably pornography. The internet has made pornography more accessible, more extreme, and more anonymous than at any other time in human history. It is a multi-billion dollar industry built on the objectification of human beings. It trains the brain to see people not as whole persons to be loved, but as a collection of body parts to be used for gratification. It rewires the brain's reward system, creating an addiction to novelty and extremity that no real-life partner can ever compete with. It is a secret, digital form of infidelity that erodes intimacy, destroys trust, and creates a profound sense of alienation between partners. (Deepfake AI will take this to a next level that we are ill-prepared for.)

Third, we have fallen for the lie of **moral licensing**. This is the psychological trick we play on ourselves that says, "Because I am a good person in other areas of my life, I am entitled to a little bit of bad behaviour in this area." Or, "My partner is not meeting my needs, so I am justified in seeking to have them met elsewhere." This is the logic of the self-serving narrative. It is the story we tell ourselves to make our betrayals seem reasonable, to make our selfishness seem like self-care. It is the ultimate refusal to take responsibility for our own commitments.

These cultural forces have created a perfect storm for the erosion of fidelity. They have made it easier than ever to cheat, and harder than ever to stay committed. The Seventh Commandment stands in stark opposition to all of this. It is a radical, counter-cultural declaration that our promises matter, that our bodies are not just instruments of pleasure, and that our relationships are not disposable commodities. It is a call to resist the logic of the market and to embrace the logic of the covenant.

Covenant vs. Contract: The Heart of the Matter

At the heart of our modern confusion about fidelity is a failure to understand the difference between a **covenant** and a **contract**. We have come to see marriage as a contract, and this is a fatal error.

A contract is a legal agreement between two self-interested parties. It is based on mutual suspicion. It says, "I will do my part as long as you do yours." It is a list of terms and conditions, of rights and responsibilities. If one party fails to uphold their end of the bargain, the other party is released from their obligations. A contract is about protecting yourself.

A covenant is something else entirely. It is a sacred, unconditional promise. It is based on mutual trust and self-giving love. It says, "I am yours, no matter what." It is not about terms and conditions; it is about a total gift of self. A covenant is not broken by the failure of one party; it is only broken when one party abandons the relationship altogether. A covenant is about giving yourself away.

The biblical understanding of marriage is that it is a covenant, not a contract. It is a reflection of the covenant relationship between God and his people. Throughout the Old Testament, God remains faithful to Israel, even when Israel is unfaithful to him. The prophet Hosea is commanded to marry a prostitute to be a living parable of God's relentless, pursuing, covenant love for his unfaithful people. This is the (symbolic) model for marriage. It is a relationship of radical, unconditional, self-giving love. And the fact that this is so hard to grasp for the modern audience is further evidence of how far we have strayed.

When we see marriage as a contract, we are constantly keeping score. We are always asking, "Am I getting a good deal? Are my needs being met? Is my partner holding up their end of the bargain?" This is a recipe for misery. It turns marriage into a power struggle, a battle of wills. It makes us insecure, anxious, and resentful.

When we see marriage as a covenant, we are free from the burden of score-keeping. We are free to love our partner without reservation, to forgive them when they fail, to serve them without expecting anything in return. This is not a recipe for being a doormat. It is a recipe for a deep, abiding, and resilient love. It is the only foundation upon which a lifelong partnership can be built.

The Law of Fidelity as a System of Order

The commandment against adultery is not just about sex. It is about the fundamental importance of keeping our promises. It is about the idea that a society can only function if its members can trust each other to do what they say they will do. And the marriage covenant is the most foundational promise of all. It is the bedrock upon which families are built, and families are the bedrock upon which societies are built.

When the marriage covenant is treated as optional, the entire social structure is weakened. Children grow up in a climate of instability and insecurity. Trust is eroded, not just between partners, but between generations. The psychological and social costs are immense. A society with high rates of family breakdown is a society with higher rates of crime, poverty, and mental illness. This is not a moralistic judgment; it is a sociological fact.

In their book *The Case for Marriage*, Linda Waite and Maggie Gallagher summarize decades of research showing that married people are, on average, healthier, wealthier, and happier than their unmarried counterparts. Their children do better in school, are less likely to be involved in crime, and are more likely to form stable relationships of their own. This is not because married people are inherently better people. It is because the institution of marriage—the public, lifelong commitment to fidelity—creates a context of stability, trust, and investment that allows individuals, families, and communities to flourish.

The Seventh Commandment is a law of social order. It is a recognition that fidelity is not just a private virtue, but a public good. It is a command to protect the foundational institution of society, to honour the promises that make social life possible. It is a call to see our marriages not just as a source of personal fulfilment, but as a sacred trust, a stewardship, a contribution to the common good.

The Test: Are You Living by the Law of Fidelity?

It is easy to condemn the obvious betrayals of an Ashley Madison or a secret affair. It is harder to see the subtle ways we may be eroding the foundations of fidelity in our own lives. Here are some diagnostic questions to consider:

- **Do you see your romantic relationships as covenants or contracts?** Are you keeping score? Are you focused on your rights, or on your responsibilities? Are you looking for a way out, or are you all in?

- **Where are you investing your emotional and sexual energy?** Are you nurturing your primary relationship, or are you diverting that energy into online flirtations, pornography, or emotional affairs?

- **Are you honest with yourself about your motivations?** Are you using the language of "self-care" to justify selfishness? Are you blaming your partner for your own failures of commitment?

- **Are you consuming media that glorifies infidelity?** Do you watch shows, read books, or listen to music that treats adultery as a glamorous or exciting adventure? How is that shaping your desires?

- **Are you building a culture of fidelity in your own life?** Do you speak with honour about your partner? Do you refuse to participate in gossip about other people's relationships? Do you model what it means to be a trustworthy and committed person?

Conclusion: The Freedom of Fidelity

We live in a culture that sees fidelity as a restriction, a cage, a limitation on our freedom. But this is a profound misunderstanding of the nature of freedom. True freedom is not the absence of constraints; it is the presence of the right constraints. A fish is not free when it is flopping on the beach; it is free when it is constrained by the banks of a river. A musician is not free when they are hitting random notes; they are free when they are constrained by the structure of a symphony.

Fidelity is a liberating constraint. It frees us from the exhausting cognitive load of deception. It frees us from the corrosive anxiety of jealousy and insecurity. It frees us from the endless, fruitless search for the perfect partner. It frees us to invest all of our energy, all of our creativity, all of our love, in one person, in one relationship, in one life.

This is the paradox of the Seventh Commandment. The law that seems to restrict our freedom is, in fact, the very thing that makes true freedom possible. It is the riverbank that allows the water of love to flow deep and strong. It is the musical scale that allows the melody of intimacy to be played.

In the end, the choice for fidelity is a choice for life. It is a choice for a life of integrity, of peace, of trust, of deep, abiding joy. It is a choice to build something beautiful and lasting in a world of disposable pleasures. It is a choice to honour the sacred neurochemistry of the bond, to protect the foundational institution of society, and to live in the freedom of the truth.

It is a choice to keep our promises. And in a world of broken promises, that may be the most radical, and the most life-giving, choice of all.

The Neuroscience of Jealousy: The Dark Side of the Bond

There is another dimension to the neurobiology of fidelity that we must confront: the experience of jealousy. If oxytocin and vasopressin are the chemicals of bonding, they are also the chemicals of mate-guarding. The same neural circuits that make us feel deeply connected to our partner also make us acutely sensitive to any threat to that connection. This is the evolutionary logic of the pair-bond: if you have invested heavily in one relationship, you have a powerful incentive to protect it.

Jealousy is often dismissed as a petty or irrational emotion, a sign of insecurity or possessiveness. But from a neurobiological perspective, it is a predictable and even adaptive response to a genuine threat. When we perceive that our partner is directing their attention, affection, or sexual interest towards someone else, our brain's threat-detection system goes into overdrive. The amygdala, the brain's alarm bell, is activated. Stress hormones flood the system. We experience a cocktail of emotions: fear, anger, anxiety, and a desperate need to reassert the bond.

This is not to say that all expressions of jealousy are healthy or justified. Pathological jealousy, driven by deep insecurity or past trauma, can become controlling, abusive, and destructive. But the baseline experience of jealousy—the discomfort we feel when our partner's attention is diverted—is not a character flaw. It is a feature of the bonding system.

It is the brain's way of saying, "This relationship matters. Protect it."

The Seventh Commandment recognises this reality. It acknowledges that the pair-bond is fragile, that it must be actively protected, and that the pain of betrayal is not just emotional but neurological. It is a command to honour the vulnerability of the bond, to resist the temptation to introduce rival signals into the system, and to recognise that our actions have profound consequences for the person we have promised to love.

The Path Forward: Rebuilding Fidelity in a Broken World

If we live in a culture that is hostile to fidelity, what can we do? How do we rebuild a culture of commitment in a world of broken promises? The answer is that we must start with ourselves. We must make the choice, every day, to live by the Law of Fidelity. We must resist the cultural currents that would sweep us away, and we must model what it means to be a person of integrity and commitment.

This begins with a radical honesty about our own desires and temptations. We must acknowledge that we are all vulnerable to infidelity, that the capacity for betrayal lives in every human heart. We must not be naïve about the power of sexual desire, the allure of novelty, or the seductive logic of the self-serving narrative. We must be vigilant, not in a spirit of fear or paranoia, but in a spirit of realism and humility.

This also requires us to invest in our primary relationships. Fidelity is not just about what we don't do; it is about what we do. It is about actively nurturing the bond, about prioritising our partner, about creating rituals of connection and intimacy. It is about having the difficult conversations, about working through conflict, about choosing to love even when we don't feel like it. It is about recognising that the grass is not greener on the other side; it is greener where you water it.

Finally, this requires us to build communities of accountability and support. We cannot do this alone. We need friends who will challenge us, who will call us out when we are drifting, who will remind us of our commitments. We need mentors who have walked this path before us, who can show us what a lifelong, faithful marriage looks like. We need a church, a community, a culture that celebrates fidelity and mourns betrayal, that holds up the covenant as the ideal and refuses to settle for the contract.

The Seventh Commandment is not just a prohibition. It is an invitation. It is an invitation to a life of deep, abiding, and resilient love. It is an invitation to build something beautiful and lasting in a world of disposable pleasures. It is an invitation to honour the sacred neurochemistry of the bond, to protect the foundational institution of society, and to live in the freedom of the truth. It is an invitation to keep our promises. And that, in the end, is the most radical and life-giving choice we can make.

The Christian Vision: Marriage as a Sacrament

For the Christian, the Law of Fidelity is not just a matter of social order or personal well-being. It is a matter of theology. Marriage, in the Christian tradition, is a **sacrament**—a visible sign of an invisible grace. It is a living parable of the relationship between Christ and the Church. As the Apostle Paul writes in Ephesians, "Husbands, love your wives, just as Christ loved the church and gave himself up for her" (Ephesians 5:25). This is a staggering claim. It means that every Christian marriage is meant to be a window into the self-giving, sacrificial, covenant love of God.

This is why adultery is not just a personal failure, but a theological one. It is a distortion of the image of God's love. It is a lie about the nature of the covenant. When a husband betrays his wife, he is not just breaking a promise to her; he is misrepresenting the character of Christ. When a wife abandons her husband, she is not just causing him pain; she is obscuring the faithfulness of God. This is a sobering reality. It means that our marriages matter not just to us, but to the world. They are a witness, for good or for ill, to the reality of God's love.

But this also means that our marriages are not just our own. They are sustained by the grace of God. We do not have to rely on our own strength, our own willpower, our own capacity for love. We can draw on the infinite resources of God's love. We can ask for his help, his healing, his transformation. We can confess our failures, receive his forgiveness, and start again. This is the good news of the gospel: that even when we have broken our promises, God has not broken his. Even when we have been unfaithful, he remains faithful. And he invites us, again and again, to return to the path of fidelity, to rebuild what has been broken, and to live in the freedom of his love.

Chapter 8: Lex Proprietatis - The Law of Property

You shall not steal. (Exodus 20:15)

In the late 1960s, a young man from Queens named Bernie Madoff began his career on Wall Street. He wasn't one of the old-money, Ivy League elite. He was the son of a plumber, a graduate of a second-tier law school, and he started his investment firm with a few thousand dollars he'd saved from working as a lifeguard and installing sprinkler systems. His firm, Bernard L. Madoff Investment Securities, was a small, scrappy operation. But Madoff was ambitious, and he had a revolutionary idea. He wanted to use new computer technology to create a more efficient, more democratic market, a third way between the buttoned-up New York Stock Exchange and the wild west of the over-the-counter market. He was, in many ways, one of the pioneers of the electronic trading system that would eventually become the NASDAQ.

By the 1980s, Madoff was a titan of Wall Street. He was respected, admired, even revered. His firm was handling a huge volume of trades, and he was seen as an innovator, a market-maker, a man who had built a financial empire from scratch. But it was his other business, his private wealth management firm, that made him a legend. It was a secret, exclusive club. You couldn't just walk in off the street and give Madoff your money. You had to be invited. And the people who were invited were a who's who of the rich and powerful: celebrities, CEOs, charities, and even other banks. The reason for the exclusivity was simple: the returns were too good to be true. Year after year, in good markets and in bad, Madoff's fund delivered steady, consistent, spectacular returns of 10 to 12 percent. It was the holy grail of investing: high returns with low risk.

For decades, the money poured in. People mortgaged their homes, emptied their retirement accounts, and convinced their friends and family to invest. They trusted Bernie. He was a pillar of the community, a philanthropist, a former chairman of the NASDAQ. He was the safest pair of hands on Wall Street. But it was all a lie. The greatest, most audacious, and most destructive lie in the history of finance.

There was no secret trading strategy. There were no brilliant investments. There was just a simple, old-fashioned Ponzi scheme. Madoff was taking money from new investors to pay off the old ones. The account statements, showing a steady stream of profitable trades, were pure fiction, printed on an old IBM computer in his office. The whole thing was a house of cards, and on December 11, 2008, in the midst of the global financial crisis, it all came crashing down.

Madoff confessed to his sons, who immediately went to the authorities. The next day, the FBI walked into his office and arrested him. The news sent a shockwave through the financial world. The losses were staggering: an estimated $65 billion in paper wealth had simply vanished. But the real cost was not financial. It was the human cost. People lost their life savings, their homes, their dreams. Charities went bankrupt. Families were torn apart. At least two people, overwhelmed by their losses, took their own lives. The man they had trusted, the man they had believed in, had not just lost their money. He had stolen it. He had stolen their past, their present, and their future.

The Madoff scandal is a story about greed, deception, and the catastrophic failure of regulatory oversight. But at its heart, it is a story about the Eighth Commandment. It is a story about what happens when we violate the fundamental law of property, when we treat what belongs to others as if it is our own. It is a story that forces us to ask: why is stealing so wrong? What is it about property that is so essential to human flourishing? And what are the subtle, modern ways that we violate this ancient law, often without even realising it?

The Psychology of "Mine": The Endowment Effect

To understand the profound violation of theft, we must first understand the profound psychology of ownership. Why do we feel so strongly about our possessions? Why does losing something feel so much worse than not gaining something of equal value? The answer lies in a powerful cognitive bias known as the **endowment effect**.

In a classic 1991 paper, the psychologists Daniel Kahneman, Jack Knetsch, and Richard Thaler described a series of simple but ingenious experiments. In one, they gave half the participants in a room a coffee mug. They then asked those who had the mugs how much they would be willing to sell it for. And they asked those who didn't have a mug how much they would be willing to pay for one. According to standard economic theory, the prices should have been roughly the same. But they weren't. Not even close. On average, the sellers demanded more than twice as much to give up their mug as the buyers were willing to pay to acquire it.

This is the endowment effect in action. The mere fact of owning something, even for a few minutes, makes us value it more highly. Kahneman and his colleagues argued that this is a manifestation of a deeper psychological principle: **loss aversion**. Our brains are wired to feel the pain of a loss more acutely than the pleasure of a gain. Losing $100 feels much worse than gaining $100 feels good. When we own something, giving it up is experienced as a loss. When we don't own it, acquiring it is experienced as a gain. And because losses loom larger than gains, we demand more to give something up than we are willing to pay to get it.

This is not just a quirk of human psychology. It is a fundamental building block of our social and economic lives. The endowment effect is what makes stable markets possible. If we didn't value what we have more than what we don't, we would be constantly trading, and the world would be a chaotic, unpredictable bazaar. The sense of "mine" is what creates stability, what allows us to plan for the future, what gives us a sense of security in a chaotic world.

Without a sense of belonging that flows from this commandment, how would we be able to experience belonging of any kind?

The Eighth Commandment, then, is not just a legal or moral injunction. It is a psychological one. It is a recognition of the deep, intuitive, and powerful sense of ownership that is wired into our brains. To steal from someone is not just to deprive them of an object. It is to violate their sense of self, to trigger the powerful, aversive machinery of loss aversion, to inflict a deep and personal wound. It is to say, "Your sense of 'mine' does not matter. Your world is not secure. I can take what is yours whenever I want." This is an act of profound psychological violence.

The Brain's Fairness Detector: The Outrage of Injustice

But the violation of theft goes even deeper. It is not just that we don't like to lose things. It is that we have a powerful, innate, and deeply emotional reaction to unfairness. Our brains are not just calculators of utility; they are detectors of injustice. And when they detect it, they sound the alarm.

In a groundbreaking 2018 study, a team of neuroscientists led by Mirre Stallen investigated the brain's response to social injustice. They had participants play a game in which they could punish someone who had treated another person unfairly. What they found was that the decision to punish was associated with a surge of activity in a specific brain region: the **anterior insula**. This is the same part of the brain that is activated when we experience physical pain, when we are exposed to a disgusting smell, or when we feel a sense of moral outrage. It is the brain's "that's not right" centre.

The anterior insula is a key hub in the brain's salience network. Its job is to monitor the world for things that are important, things that we need to pay attention to. And one of the most important things it pays attention to is fairness. When we see someone being treated unfairly, when we see someone's property being taken from them, our anterior insula lights up. We feel a visceral, emotional reaction. We feel outrage. We feel a powerful motivation to restore justice, to punish the transgressor, to make things right.

This is the neurobiological root of our hatred of theft. It is not just a rational calculation that theft is bad for society. It is a deep, emotional, and intuitive conviction that it is wrong. The Eighth Commandment is not just a good idea; it is a reflection of the way our brains are wired. We are hardwired for fairness. We are hardwired to believe that people should not take what does not belong to them. To steal is to violate this fundamental, biologically encoded social grammar.

The Modern Faces of Theft: A Taxonomy of Taking

The Eighth Commandment is simple and direct: "You shall not steal." But in the modern world, theft has become complex and indirect. It is often hidden behind layers of bureaucracy, disguised in the fine print of a contract, or laundered through complex financial instruments. But it is still theft. And its consequences are just as devastating.

First, there is the pervasive and often invisible crime of **wage theft**. This is what happens when employers fail to pay their workers what they are legally owed. It can take many forms: paying less than the minimum wage, refusing to pay overtime, forcing workers to work off the clock, or misclassifying employees as independent contractors to avoid paying benefits. According to the Economic Policy Institute, more than $1.5 billion in stolen wages were recovered for workers in the United States between 2021 and 2023. And this is just the tip of the iceberg. The total amount of wage theft is estimated to be in the tens of billions of dollars per year, far exceeding the value of all other forms of property crime combined. This is not a rounding error. It is a massive, systemic transfer of wealth from the pockets of working people to the balance sheets of their employers. It is theft on an industrial scale.

Second, there is the sophisticated and often celebrated crime of **corporate theft**. This is the world of Bernie Madoff, of

Enron, of the 2008 financial crisis. It is the world of accounting fraud, of insider trading, of predatory lending, of market manipulation. It is the world where theft is disguised as "aggressive accounting," "financial innovation," or "shareholder value." It is a world where the sums are so large, and the methods so complex, that we can become numb to the reality of the crime. But the consequences are real. People lose their jobs, their homes, their pensions. Entire economies are brought to their knees. And the fabric of social trust is torn apart.

Third, there is the ubiquitous and often trivialised crime of **intellectual property theft**. In the digital age, it has become trivially easy to copy and distribute creative work without permission. Music, movies, software, books—all can be downloaded with the click of a button. We tell ourselves that it's a victimless crime, that the big corporations can afford it, that information wants to be free. But this is a self-serving narrative. For the artist, the writer, the musician, the software developer, their work is their property. It is the fruit of their labour, the product of their creativity. To take it without permission is to devalue their work, to undermine their livelihood, and to disincentivise the creation of new and beautiful things. It is to say that their labour has no value, that their property has no rights.

These are just a few of the modern faces of theft. But they all have one thing in common. They are all violations of the Eighth Commandment. They are all a refusal to respect the fundamental right of others to own and enjoy the fruits of their labour. They are all a manifestation of the ancient, destructive impulse to take what is not ours.

The Ripple Effects: How Theft Destroys Social Trust

The harm of theft extends far beyond the immediate victim. Every act of theft sends a signal through the social network, a message that the rules do not apply, that trust is foolish, that everyone must look out for themselves. This is the hidden, corrosive cost of theft: it destroys the fabric of social trust that makes cooperation possible.

Consider the aftermath of the Madoff scandal. It wasn't just the direct victims who were harmed. It was the entire financial system. In the wake of the revelation, investors became more suspicious, more risk-averse, more reluctant to trust anyone with their money. The cost of capital went up. New businesses struggled to find funding. The economy contracted. The ripple effects of Madoff's theft were felt by millions of people who had never heard of him, who had never invested a dollar with him. This is the nature of theft in a complex, interconnected economy. It is not a zero-sum transfer of wealth from one person to another. It is a negative-sum destruction of value that harms everyone.

This is why societies invest so heavily in systems of law enforcement, in courts, in prisons. It is not just about punishing the guilty. It is about maintaining the social trust that makes economic life possible. When theft goes unpunished, when the rule of law breaks down, the result is not just a transfer of wealth from the law-abiding to the lawless. It is a collapse of the entire system of cooperation. People stop investing. They stop trading. They stop trusting. The economy grinds to a halt. This is the lesson of every failed state, of every society that has descended into chaos. The protection of property rights is not a luxury. It is a necessity.

The Law of Property as a System of Order

The Eighth Commandment is not just a moral injunction. It is a law of economic and social order. A society that does not protect private property is a society that cannot create wealth. This is one of the most important and well-established findings in the history of economics.

In his groundbreaking book *The Mystery of Capital*, the Peruvian economist Hernando de Soto asked a simple question: why do some countries prosper while others remain mired in poverty? His answer was that the key difference is the presence of a formal, legally protected system of private property rights. In the West, he argued, most property is formally registered. It has a title, a deed, a legal address. This allows it to be used as collateral for a loan, to be bought and sold in a market, to be invested in a business. It allows capital to be created.

In many developing countries, by contrast, most property is held informally. People may live in a house or farm a piece of land for generations, but they have no legal title to it. Their property is what de Soto calls "dead capital." It cannot be used to create wealth. It cannot be leveraged to build a better future. The result is a society trapped in a low-trust, low-growth equilibrium. Without secure property rights, there is no incentive to invest, to improve, to build for the long term. Why would you build a house if someone can come and take it from you tomorrow? Why would you plant a field if you have no guarantee that you will be able to harvest the crop? A society without property rights is a society without a future.

De Soto's insight is profound because it reveals that the problem of poverty is not primarily a problem of resources. The poor in many developing countries are not poor because they lack assets. They are poor because they lack the legal infrastructure to turn those assets into capital. They have land, they have houses, they have businesses. But they cannot use them to secure a loan, to attract investment, to build wealth. The Eighth Commandment, then, is not just a moral principle. It is an economic necessity. A society that does not protect property rights is a society that condemns its people to perpetual poverty.

The Eighth Commandment is the foundation of a prosperous and flourishing society. It is the legal and moral bedrock upon which the entire edifice of the market economy is built. It is the law that says, "What is yours is yours, and what is mine is mine." It is the law that allows us to trust each other, to cooperate with each other, to build a world of mutual benefit and shared prosperity. To violate this law is not just to harm an individual. It is to undermine the very foundations of civilisation.

The Christian Vision: Stewardship over Ownership

For the Christian, the Law of Property is both affirmed and transformed. It is affirmed in its recognition of the importance of private property, of the right of individuals to own and enjoy the fruits of their labour. But it is transformed by a deeper and more radical understanding of the nature of ownership. In the Christian vision, we are not ultimate owners. We are stewards.

The Bible begins with the declaration that "the earth is the Lord's, and everything in it" (Psalm 24:1). We are not the creators of the world; we are its caretakers. We have been given a temporary and conditional grant of authority over a small portion of God's creation. We are managers, not owners. And one day, we will be called to give an account of our stewardship.

This changes everything. It means that our property is not ultimately for us. It is for God, and for the flourishing of his creation. It is a tool to be used, not a treasure to be hoarded. It is a resource to be invested in the work of justice, of mercy, of compassion. The question is not, "How much can I accumulate?" but "How can I use what I have been given to love God and to love my neighbour?"

This vision of stewardship is a powerful critique of both the excesses of capitalism and the illusions of socialism. Against the capitalist who says, "It's my money, and I can do whatever I want with it," the Christian says, "It's not your money. It's God's money. And you have a responsibility to use it for his purposes." Against the socialist who says, "Private property is theft," the Christian says, "Private property is a sacred trust, a stewardship, a responsibility."

The Eighth Commandment, seen through the lens of stewardship, is not just a command not to steal from our neighbour. It is a command to actively use what we have for the good of our neighbour. It is a command to be generous, to be compassionate, to be just. It is a command to see our property not as a source of security, but as an instrument of service.

This is why the biblical law goes far beyond a simple prohibition on theft. It includes positive commands to care for the poor, to leave the edges of the field unharvested so that the widow and the orphan can glean, to forgive debts every seven years, to return land to its original owners every fifty years in the Year of Jubilee. These are not optional acts of charity. They are legal requirements, built into the very structure of the economic system. They are a recognition that property is not an absolute right, but a conditional stewardship. They are a safeguard against the concentration of wealth and power, a mechanism for ensuring that everyone has access to the resources they need to flourish.

In the New Testament, this vision of stewardship becomes even more radical. Jesus tells the rich young ruler to sell everything he has and give to the poor. He says that it is easier for a camel to go through the eye of a needle than for a rich person to enter the kingdom of God. He tells the parable of the rich fool, who builds bigger barns to store his wealth, only to die that very night. The early church in Jerusalem practises a form of voluntary communal living, where "no one claimed that any of their possessions was their own, but they shared everything they had" (Acts 4:32). This is not a command for all Christians at all times, but it is a powerful vision of what it looks like to take the principle of stewardship seriously.

The Christian vision of property, then, is a vision of radical generosity, of sacrificial love, of a willingness to use what we have for the good of others. It is a vision that stands in stark contrast to the greed and selfishness of our age. It is a vision that calls us to a higher standard, to a life of service and self-giving. It is a vision that recognises that the Eighth Commandment is not just about what we don't do (steal), but about what we do (give, share, serve).

The Paradox of Generosity: Why Giving Makes Us Richer

There is a profound paradox at the heart of the Law of Property. The more we give away, the richer we become. Not necessarily in material terms, though even that is sometimes true. But certainly in the things that matter most: in relationships, in meaning, in joy, in peace. This is not just a spiritual truth. It is a psychological one.

Research on the psychology of giving has consistently found that people who are generous are happier, healthier, and more satisfied with their lives than those who are not. In one study, participants were given a sum of money and told to either spend it on themselves or on someone else. Those who spent it on others reported significantly higher levels of happiness at the end of the day than those who spent it on themselves. In another study, researchers found that people who gave money to charity activated the same reward centres in the brain that are activated when they receive money themselves. Giving, it turns out, is neurologically rewarding. It makes us feel good.

But the benefits of generosity go deeper than just a temporary boost in mood. Generous people have stronger social networks, more meaningful relationships, and a greater sense of purpose in life. They are less likely to be depressed, less likely to be anxious, and more likely to report a sense of flourishing. This is because generosity is fundamentally relational. When we give, we connect with others. We build trust. We create bonds of reciprocity and mutual care. We become part of a community. And it is in community, not in isolation, that human beings thrive.

The Eighth Commandment, then, is not just a prohibition on theft. It is an invitation to a life of generosity, a life of connection, a life of flourishing. It is an invitation to discover the paradox that the more we give away, the richer we become. It is an invitation to live not in the scarcity mindset of "mine," but in the abundance mindset of "ours." It is an invitation to build a world where property is not a source of division and conflict, but a tool for building community and creating shared prosperity.

The Test: Are You Living by the Law of Property?

It is easy to condemn the brazen theft of a Bernie Madoff or the systemic injustice of wage theft. It is harder to see the subtle ways that we may be violating the spirit of the Eighth Commandment in our own lives. Here are some diagnostic questions to consider:

- **Are you honest in your financial dealings?** Do you pay your taxes? Do you pay your debts? Do you give an honest day's work for an honest day's pay?

- **Are you generous with what you have?** Do you see your property as a resource to be shared, or as a treasure to be protected? Do you give freely to those in need, to your church, to the work of justice and mercy in the world?

- **Are you a good steward of the resources you have been given?** Are you wasteful? Are you consumed by a desire for more? Or are you content with what you have, and focused on using it for the good of others?

- **Do you respect the property of others?** Do you download copyrighted material without permission?

Do you borrow things and fail to return them? Do you take advantage of the generosity of others?

- **Are you complicit in systems of theft?** Do you invest in companies that exploit their workers? Do you buy products from companies that use slave labour? Do you turn a blind eye to the injustices of the global economic system?

Conclusion: The Freedom of Stewardship

We live in a culture that is torn between two false gospels of property. The gospel of the market tells us that our property is ours to do with as we please, that the accumulation of wealth is the ultimate goal of life. The gospel of the state tells us that private property is the source of all injustice, that it must be abolished for the sake of the collective. Both of these gospels are lies. They are both violations of the deep, ancient wisdom of the Eighth Commandment.

The gospel of the market leads to a world of ruthless competition, where the strong prey on the weak, where the accumulation of wealth becomes an end in itself, where the poor are left behind. It is a world where Bernie Madoff can steal billions and be celebrated as a genius until the house of cards collapses. It is a world where wage theft is endemic, where corporations can externalise costs onto workers and communities, where the pursuit of profit justifies any means. This is not freedom. This is bondage to greed, to anxiety, to the endless treadmill of accumulation.

The gospel of the state, on the other hand, leads to a world of stagnation and oppression, where the incentive to work, to innovate, to create is destroyed, where the state becomes the arbiter of all economic activity, where the individual is subsumed into the collective. It is a world where property rights are abolished in the name of equality, but where the result is not equality but poverty. It is a world where the state, not the individual, becomes the thief, confiscating the fruits of labour in the name of the common good. This, too, is not freedom. This is bondage to ideology, to bureaucracy, to the dead hand of central planning.

The Law of Property, understood in its fullness, offers us a third way. It is the way of stewardship. It is the way that recognises the importance of private property as a foundation for human flourishing, but that also recognises that our property is not ultimately our own. It is a sacred trust, a gift from God, a tool to be used for his purposes. It is a way that affirms the right of individuals to own and enjoy the fruits of their labour, but that also insists that this right comes with responsibilities, with obligations to the poor, to the community, to the future.

This is a vision that frees us from the anxiety of accumulation and the resentment of envy. It frees us from the illusion that our security lies in our possessions, and from the lie that our worth is determined by our net worth. It frees us to be generous, to be just, to be content. It frees us to see our economic lives not as a zero-sum game of competition and conflict, but as a positive-sum game of cooperation and mutual service. It frees us to ask not "How much can I get?" but "How much can I give?" It frees us to see our neighbours not as competitors or threats, but as fellow stewards, fellow image-bearers of God, fellow travellers on the journey towards the kingdom.

In the end, the choice to live by the Law of Property is a choice for life. It is a choice for a life of integrity, of justice, of generosity, of peace. It is a choice to build a world where everyone has the opportunity to flourish, where the rights of the poor are protected, and where the gifts of creation are used for the good of all. It is a choice to be a faithful steward of the mysteries of God. And in a world of greed and injustice, that may be the most radical, and the most life-giving, choice of all.

The Eighth Commandment is not a restriction. It is a liberation. It is a call to live in the freedom of stewardship, in the joy of generosity, in the peace of contentment. It is a call to build an economy not of theft, but of trust. Not of exploitation, but of mutual service. Not of accumulation, but of stewardship. This is the vision of the Law of Property. This is the way of life.

Chapter 9: Lex Veritatis - The Law of Truth

You shall not bear false witness against your neighbour. (Exodus 20:16)

In 1974, a young cognitive psychologist named Elizabeth Loftus stumbled upon a discovery that would not only define her career but also shake the foundations of the legal system. The experiment was deceptively simple. She showed participants a series of slides depicting a car accident. The images were unremarkable, the kind of thing you might see in a driver's education manual: a red Datsun proceeds down a street, stops at a stop sign, turns right, and in the process, knocks over a pedestrian. After viewing the slides, the participants were asked a series of questions. For half of them, the critical question was: "Did another car pass the red Datsun while it was stopped at the stop sign?" For the other half, the question was subtly, almost imperceptibly, different: "Did another car pass the red Datsun while it was stopped at the yield sign?"

There was no yield sign. The slides had clearly shown a stop sign. Yet, when the participants were later asked to recall what they had seen, the power of that single, misplaced word was astonishing. A significant number of those who had been fed the "yield sign" question now remembered seeing a yield sign. Their memory, the supposedly inviolable record of their own experience, had been overwritten. A fiction had become a fact. A lie had become their truth.

This was the birth of the "misinformation effect," one of the most robust and replicated findings in all of psychology.

Loftus and her colleagues would go on to conduct hundreds of similar experiments, each one a variation on this theme of memory's malleability. They showed that it was possible to plant entirely false memories in the minds of ordinary, healthy people: vivid, detailed memories of being lost in a shopping mall as a child, of being attacked by a vicious animal, of witnessing a demonic possession. They demonstrated, with chilling clarity, that the confidence with which a memory is held has little or no correlation with its accuracy. A person can be absolutely certain that they remember something that never happened. They showed, in short, that the human mind is a deeply unreliable narrator.

The implications of this research rippled out from the psychology lab and into the real world, crashing against the bedrock assumptions of the legal system. For centuries, eyewitness testimony had been considered the gold standard of evidence. "Seeing is believing," the old saying goes. In the courtroom, there was no more powerful testimony than that of a confident witness pointing a finger and saying, "That's the man I saw." But Loftus's work revealed this faith to be tragically misplaced. Eyewitnesses are often wrong. Their memories can be contaminated by leading questions from police officers, by media reports, by conversations with other witnesses, by the very act of being asked to recall an event over and over again. The Innocence Project, a non-profit organisation that uses DNA evidence to exonerate the wrongfully convicted, has found that mistaken eyewitness identification was a factor in more than 70 percent of the cases they have overturned. That's hundreds of people who have spent years, sometimes decades, in prison for crimes they did not commit, all because of the fallibility of human memory.

The Ninth Commandment, "You shall not bear false witness against your neighbour," is not just a moral injunction against lying. It is a recognition of the profound social importance of truth, of the devastating consequences of falsehood, of the fragility of the human systems we have built to discern one from the other. It is a law that is more relevant today than ever before, in an age of misinformation, of deepfakes, of narrative warfare, an age where the very foundations of our shared reality seem to be cracking beneath our feet.

The Psychology of Deception: Why We Lie

Before we can understand the social consequences of lying, we must first understand its psychological roots. Why do people lie? The most obvious answer is for personal gain. We lie to avoid punishment, to gain an advantage, to impress others, to protect ourselves. This is what psychologists call **instrumental lying**. It is a rational, calculated act, a tool that we use to get what we want.

But there is another, more subtle, and perhaps more pervasive form of lying: **self-deception**. We lie not just to others, but to ourselves. We tell ourselves that we are smarter, or more talented, or more moral than we really are. We construct elaborate narratives to justify our failures, to rationalise our mistakes, to maintain our self-esteem. This is the world of cognitive dissonance, of motivated reasoning, of the confirmation bias. It is the world where our beliefs are not shaped by the evidence, but by our desires. (And this is necessary, because as sinful human beings, we cannot perfectly comply with Lex Proprietatis!)

And the line between self-deception and other-deception is a blurry one. The more we lie to ourselves, the easier it becomes to lie to others. The more we believe our own propaganda, the more convincing we become. The most effective liars are often the ones who have first convinced themselves that their lies are true.

This cognitive effort is not just a metaphor. It is a measurable neurological reality. Lying is hard work. It requires the brain to perform a series of complex operations simultaneously: suppressing the truth, constructing a plausible alternative, maintaining consistency with previous statements, and monitoring the other person's reactions for signs of disbelief. As deception researchers like Aldert Vrij have shown, this places a significant load on our cognitive resources, particularly our working memory. When our brains are already taxed, our ability to lie effectively plummets. This is the principle behind many modern lie-detection techniques, which seek to increase the cognitive load on a suspect in order to make it more likely that they will slip up, that the carefully constructed facade of their deception will crack under the strain.

This is the psychological soil in which the crisis of truth is rooted. It is not just that there are bad actors who are intentionally trying to deceive us. It is that we are all, to some extent, complicit in our own deception. We are all motivated to believe what we want to believe, to seek out information that confirms our biases, to live in a world of our own making. And in the modern media environment, it has never been easier to do so.

The Social Infrastructure of Truth

Human beings are a cooperative species. We are not the strongest, or the fastest, or the most ferocious animals on the planet. Our superpower is our ability to work together, to coordinate our actions, to build complex societies. And the foundation of all of this is trust. We trust that the bridge will hold, that the surgeon will be competent, that the banker will not steal our money. And the foundation of trust is truth.

Language is the primary medium through which we build and maintain this web of trust. We use language to make promises, to share information, to coordinate our behaviour. When we speak, we are not just transmitting data. We are performing a social act. We are making a claim about the world, and we are implicitly asking others to trust that our claim is true. When we bear false witness, we are not just uttering a falsehood. We are poisoning the well of social trust. We are undermining the very foundation of our cooperative existence.

This is why every society in human history has had strong norms against lying, especially in formal, public contexts like a courtroom. The act of taking an oath, of swearing to tell "the truth, the whole truth, and nothing but the truth," is a recognition of the sacred importance of testimony. It is a recognition that the justice system, and indeed the entire social order, depends on the willingness of individuals to speak truthfully, even when it is difficult or costly to do so.

When this trust breaks down, the consequences are catastrophic. A society that cannot agree on basic facts is a society that cannot solve its problems. A society where everyone is a liar is a society where no one can be trusted. A society where truth is a matter of opinion is a society on the verge of collapse. The Ninth Commandment is not just a rule for individuals. It is a law of social physics. It is the operating system of a functioning society.

The Modern Crisis of Truth

For most of human history, the primary threat to truth was the fallibility of individual human beings: the liar, the gossip, the mistaken eyewitness. But in the 21st century, we are facing a new and more insidious threat: the industrialisation of falsehood, the weaponisation of narrative, the algorithmic amplification of lies. We are living in a post-truth world, a world where the very concept of objective truth is under assault.

First, there is the crisis of **misinformation**. The internet and social media have created a media ecosystem where falsehoods can spread faster and farther than ever before. A 2018 study from MIT found that false news stories on X were 70 percent more likely to be retweeted than true stories. They spread faster, they reached more people, and they were more persistent. The researchers concluded that this was not primarily due to bots or foreign influence campaigns, but to the behaviour of ordinary human beings. We are more likely to share novel, surprising, and emotionally charged information, and falsehoods are often more novel, more surprising, and more emotionally charged than the truth.

This creates a vicious cycle. The more misinformation we are exposed to, the more we come to believe it. The more we believe it, the more we share it. The more we share it, the more it is amplified by the algorithms that are designed to maximise engagement. The result is a polluted information environment, a world where it is increasingly difficult to distinguish fact from fiction, where conspiracy theories flourish, where public trust in institutions like the media, the government, and science is in freefall.

Second, there is the looming crisis of **deepfakes**. In the last few years, advances in artificial intelligence have made it possible to create highly realistic, synthetic videos of people saying and doing things they never said or did. At the moment, it is still possible for experts to detect these fakes. But the technology is improving at an exponential rate. We are rapidly approaching a world where it will be impossible to distinguish a real video from a fake one. A world where, as the saying goes, we will not be able to believe our own eyes.

The potential for malicious use of this technology is terrifying. Imagine a deepfake video of a political candidate admitting to a crime, released on the eve of an election. Imagine a deepfake video of a CEO announcing a fake bankruptcy, causing a stock market crash. Imagine a deepfake video of a military commander issuing a false order, triggering a war. This is not science fiction. This is the world we are about to inhabit. It is a world where the very concept of evidence is thrown into question, where the potential for deception and manipulation is almost limitless.

Third, there is the crisis of **narrative warfare**. In a polarised society, information is no longer a tool for understanding the world. It is a weapon to be used against one's enemies. We are no longer engaged in a shared search for truth. We are engaged in a zero-sum struggle for narrative dominance. Each side has its own facts, its own experts, its own media ecosystem. Each side sees the other not as mistaken, but as evil. Each side believes that it is fighting for the soul of the nation, that the stakes are existential, that any means are justified to achieve victory.

This is the world of "alternative facts," of "whataboutism," of "fake news." It is a world where the goal is not to persuade, but to demoralise, to confuse, to overwhelm. It is a world where the line between journalism and activism has been erased, where the media is no longer a watchdog, but a lapdog. It is a world where we are all soldiers in a culture war, and where truth is the first casualty.

Nowhere was this more horrifically demonstrated than in Rwanda in 1994. The genocide of the Tutsi was not a spontaneous eruption of ancient tribal hatreds. It was a meticulously planned and executed campaign of extermination, and its primary weapon was narrative. For years leading up to the genocide, Hutu extremist media, particularly the infamous radio station Radio Télévision Libre des Mille Collines (RTLM), broadcast a constant stream of propaganda that dehumanised the Tutsi minority. They were not neighbours, friends, or fellow citizens. They were "cockroaches" (inyenzi), "snakes," a foreign infestation that needed to be cleansed from the body politic. The radio hosts, with their casual, conversational style, would read out the names and addresses of Tutsi families, marking them for death. They created a narrative in which violence was not a crime, but a patriotic duty, a form of community service. They bore false witness on an industrial scale, and the result was the murder of 800,000 people in 100 days. This is the ultimate end of narrative warfare: not just a society that cannot agree on facts, but a society that slaughters its own people.

The Internal Exile: The Psychological Cost of a Post-Truth World

The consequences of a post-truth world are not just social and political. They are deeply personal. To live in a world saturated with falsehood is to live in a state of constant, low-grade anxiety. It is to be unmoored from reality, adrift in a sea of conflicting narratives, unable to trust the ground beneath your own feet. This is the psychological cost of bearing false witness on a societal scale: it creates a culture of cynicism, paranoia, and existential dread.

When we can no longer trust our institutions, our leaders, or even our own senses, we become chronically suspicious. Every statement is scrutinised for its hidden motive, every event is a potential conspiracy. This is not a healthy skepticism. It is a corrosive cynicism that eats away at our ability to form trusting relationships, to engage in meaningful dialogue, to feel at home in the world. We become, in a sense, exiles in our own society, unable to connect with others because the very medium of connection—shared truth—has been contaminated.

This external chaos inevitably creates an internal one. **Our sense of self is a narrative, a story that we tell ourselves about who we are, where we have come from, and where we are going. This story is built on a foundation of memories, beliefs, and values. When that foundation is shaken, when we are told that our memories are unreliable, that our beliefs are just a product of our biases, that our values are relative, our sense of self begins to crumble. We are left with a fragmented, incoherent identity, a collection of conflicting impulses and desires with no unifying centre. This is the spiritual crisis at the heart of the post-truth condition: a loss of the very idea of a stable, integrated self.**

In this state of internal exile, we become more susceptible to the simplistic, black-and-white narratives of extremism. When we have no story of our own, we are more likely to be captured by the story of a demagogue, a cult leader, a conspiracy theorist. When we have no stable identity, we are more likely to find a sense of belonging in the tribalism of identity politics. The void of truth is filled by the certainty of ideology. The chaos of relativism is replaced by the tyranny of absolutism. This is the terrible paradox of the post-truth world: in our flight from the constraints of truth, we have not found freedom, but a new and more terrible form of bondage.

The Christian Vision: Truth as a Person

For the Christian, the crisis of truth is not just a social or political problem. It is a theological one. The Bible is a book that is obsessed with truth. The word "truth" appears hundreds of times in its pages. But the biblical understanding of truth is different from the modern, secular one. In the modern view, truth is a property of statements, a correspondence between language and reality. In the biblical view, truth is a property of persons. It is about faithfulness, about reliability, about trustworthiness. God is true not (only) because his statements are accurate, but because he is faithful to his promises, because he is who he says he is.

This is why, in the Gospel of John, Jesus does not say, "I will teach you the truth." He says, "I am the way, the truth, and the life." For the Christian, truth is not a set of propositions. It is a person. It is the (perfect) person of Jesus Christ, who is the perfect image of the invisible God, the one in whom all the promises of God find their "Yes." To know the truth is not to master a set of facts. It is to be in a relationship with a person.

This personal, relational understanding of truth is rooted in the Hebrew concept of *emet*, which is often translated as "truth," but which carries a much richer set of meanings:

faithfulness, reliability, steadfastness, integrity. When the psalmist says that God's *emet* endures to all generations, he is not merely making a statement about the accuracy of God's propositions. He is making a statement about the reliability of God's character. God is true because he is trustworthy, because He always keeps his promises, because He is faithful to his covenant people.

This is a profound challenge to our modern, disembodied, and often cynical understanding of truth. We have come to see truth as a commodity, a resource to be mined, a weapon to be wielded. But the Bible reminds us that truth is covenantal. It is the foundation of relationship, the currency of community, the lifeblood of love. To speak the truth is to honour the image of God in our neighbour. To lie is to desecrate it.

This has profound implications for how we think about the Ninth Commandment. To bear false witness is not just to make an inaccurate statement. It is to be unfaithful to our neighbour. It is to break the bonds of trust that hold us together in community. It is to act in a way that is contrary to the very character of God.

This is why the Bible is so uncompromising in its condemnation of lying. "The Lord detests lying lips," says the book of Proverbs, "but he delights in people who are trustworthy." The book of Revelation says that "all liars" will have their place in the lake of fire. This is not because God is an obsessive-compulsive fact-checker. It is because lying is a form of spiritual violence. It is a denial of the image of God in our neighbour. It is a participation in the work of the one whom Jesus called "the father of lies."

The Role of Institutions: Guardians of Truth

While individual commitment to truth is essential, it is not sufficient. The social infrastructure of truth requires institutions: courts, universities, media organisations, scientific bodies, religious communities. These are the guardians of truth, the custodians of the collective memory, the arbiters of what counts as knowledge. When these institutions function well, they create a stable epistemic environment, a shared reality in which rational discourse and collective problem-solving are possible. When they fail, the consequences are catastrophic.

Consider the role of the **judiciary**. The entire legal system is predicated on the assumption that it is possible to determine, with reasonable confidence, what actually happened in a given case. This is why we have rules of evidence, why we require witnesses to take oaths, why we have adversarial proceedings in which both sides present their case and a neutral arbiter makes a judgment. The goal is not perfect certainty—that is impossible—but a reasonable approximation of the truth, arrived at through a transparent and fair process. When this system works, justice is served. When it fails, when witnesses lie, when evidence is fabricated, when judges are corrupt, the result is not just individual injustice, but a loss of faith in the entire system. People stop believing that the law is fair, that the courts can be trusted, that there is any point in seeking justice through official channels. They take matters into their own hands. Vigilantism replaces the rule of law. Might makes right.

Consider the role of the **university**. The modern research university is one of humanity's greatest inventions, a place where knowledge is not just transmitted, but created, where the next generation of scholars is trained, where difficult questions are asked and rigorous methods are applied to find answers. The university is not perfect—it is subject to all the usual human failings of bias, careerism, and groupthink—but at its best, it is a place where truth is valued above all else, where intellectual honesty is the highest virtue, where the goal is not to win an argument, but to get closer to reality. When universities abandon this mission, when they become ideological echo chambers, when they prioritise political correctness over intellectual rigor, they betray their fundamental purpose. They cease to be guardians of truth and become purveyors of propaganda.

Consider the role of the **media**. In a democracy, the media is often called the "fourth estate," a check on the power of government, a watchdog that holds the powerful accountable. This requires a commitment to truth, to accuracy, to fairness. It requires journalists who see their role not as activists or entertainers, but as seekers of truth, who are willing to follow the evidence wherever it leads, even when it contradicts their own biases or the interests of their employers. When the media fails in this mission, when it becomes a mouthpiece for a political party, when it prioritises clicks and outrage over accuracy and nuance, it ceases to be a guardian of truth and becomes a threat to democracy itself.

These institutions are fragile. They require constant vigilance, constant renewal, constant recommitment to their founding principles. They require individuals within them who are willing to put truth above tribe, who are willing to speak up when they see falsehood, who are willing to pay the cost of integrity. And they require a broader culture that values and supports them, that recognises their importance, that is willing to defend them against those who would corrupt or destroy them.

The Path Forward: Living in the Truth

How, then, are we to live in a post-truth world? How are we to be people of the truth in an age of lies? The Ninth Commandment offers us a path forward, a set of practices for cultivating a life of truthfulness.

First, we must be **committed to the truth in our own speech**. This is the personal, daily practice of integrity. It means more than just avoiding outright lies. It means cultivating a deep respect for the power of words. It means being precise in our language, choosing our words carefully, and striving for accuracy in all that we say. It means resisting the temptation to exaggerate for effect, to round up the numbers, to add a little bit of spice to a story to make it more entertaining. It means refusing to participate in gossip, which is a form of bearing false witness against our neighbour in a casual, everyday context. It means being willing to say "I don't know" when we don't know, rather than pretending to have an expertise we don't possess. It means being quick to admit when we are wrong, to apologise for our mistakes, to correct the record. It means, in short, being people of our word, people whose "yes" means "yes" and whose "no" means "no." This is not a small thing. In a world of spin and hype, a person who can be trusted to speak the plain, unvarnished truth is a rock in a sea of uncertainty.

Second, we must be **critical consumers of information**. In the modern media environment, this is a non-negotiable survival skill. It means developing a healthy skepticism, not a corrosive cynicism. It means understanding that all information is mediated, that it comes to us through a filter, whether that filter is a journalist, a social media influencer, or an algorithm. It means being aware of our own biases, particularly the confirmation bias, our tendency to seek out and believe information that confirms our existing beliefs. It means actively seeking out a wide range of sources, especially sources that challenge our own perspective, that make us uncomfortable, that force us to think. It means learning to recognise the hallmarks of misinformation: emotionally charged language, appeals to fear and outrage, a lack of sources, a refusal to engage with counter-arguments. It means being willing to do the hard work of verification, of fact-checking, of slow, careful, critical thinking. It means, in the words of the old journalistic adage, "If your mother says she loves you, check it out."

Third, we must be **creators of a culture of truth**. The crisis of truth is a collective problem, and it requires a collective solution. We cannot solve it alone. We must work together to rebuild the social infrastructure of truth. This means holding our leaders accountable for their words, refusing to accept lies and distortions, regardless of their political party. It means supporting independent, high-quality journalism with our subscriptions and our attention. It means creating spaces in our homes, our churches, our communities for civil, respectful dialogue across our differences. It means modelling a different way of being in the world, a way that is characterised by intellectual humility, by curiosity, by a genuine desire to understand the other, even, and especially, when we disagree. It means being a non-anxious presence in an anxious world, a voice of reason in a sea of outrage. It means, in the language of the New Testament, "speaking the truth in love," recognising that the goal of truth is not to win an argument, but to build a relationship, to heal a wound, to restore a community.

The Test: Are You Living by the Law of Truth?

It is easy to decry the post-truth world, to lament the decline of journalistic standards, to rage against the purveyors of fake news. It is harder to examine our own relationship with the truth, to see the subtle ways that we may be contributing to the very culture of falsehood that we condemn. Here are some diagnostic questions to consider:

- **Are you a truth-teller?** Do you speak with precision and care? Do you resist the urge to exaggerate, to gossip, to pass on unverified information? Are you willing to speak the truth even when it is unpopular or costly?

- **Are you a truth-seeker?** Do you actively seek out information that challenges your own beliefs? Do you read widely, listen carefully, and think critically? Or do you retreat into the comfort of your own echo chamber, consuming only information that confirms your existing biases?

- **Are you a truth-lover?** Do you delight in the truth, even when it is uncomfortable? Do you have the humility to admit when you are wrong? Do you have the courage to change your mind in the face of new evidence?

- **Are you a truth-builder?** Do you create spaces for honest, respectful dialogue? Do you model a way of communicating that is characterised by grace and charity? Do you support institutions that are committed to the pursuit of truth, whether in journalism, in science, or in the church?

Conclusion: The Freedom of Truth

The Ninth Commandment is not a burden. It is a liberation. It is a liberation from the anxiety of having to constantly manage our image, to spin our story, to maintain our lies. It is a liberation from the cynicism and despair of a post-truth world. It is a liberation into the freedom of living in the truth, of being who we are, of saying what we mean and meaning what we say.

In the end, the choice to live by the Law of Truth is a choice for life. It is a choice for a life of integrity, of trust, of community, of peace. It is a choice to build a world where truth is not a weapon, but a bridge. A world where we can see each other not as enemies, but as fellow travellers, fellow seekers, fellow image-bearers of the God who is Truth. And in a world of lies, that may be the most radical, and the most life-giving, choice of all.

Chapter 10: Lex Contentamenti - The Law of Contentment

You Shall Not Covet

In late 2016, a single, ambiguous post appeared on the Instagram feeds of hundreds of the world's most influential social media personalities. It was a simple, solid orange square. No text, no explanation. Just a vibrant, arresting block of colour. The influencers—models like Kendall Jenner and Bella Hadid, musicians, and a legion of lesser-known but highly-followed lifestyle gurus—had all been paid, some handsomely, to post it. The coordinated drop created an immediate storm of online curiosity. What was this mysterious orange tile? What did it mean?

The answer, when it came, was a masterclass in manufacturing desire. The orange squares were the heralds of Fyre Festival, a new, ultra-exclusive music festival scheduled for the spring of 2017 on a private island in the Bahamas once owned by Pablo Escobar. The promotional video that followed was a work of art, a two-and-a-half-minute distillation of pure, unadulterated envy. It featured a squadron of supermodels frolicking on pristine white-sand beaches, riding jet skis through turquoise water, and partying on luxury yachts. It promised gourmet food, opulent villas, and intimate performances from major musical acts. It wasn't just selling a festival; it was selling a fantasy, a vision of a life so perfect, so glamorous, so effortlessly cool that it seemed to exist on a different plane of reality.

The marketing campaign was a direct injection of social comparison into the veins of millions. It was designed to make you feel that your life, right now, was drab and insufficient. It was engineered to make you *want*. And it worked. Tickets, with packages costing up to US$250,000, sold out almost instantly. People didn't just want to go to Fyre Festival; they felt they *needed* to go. They were coveting not just a ticket, but an identity—the identity of someone who belonged in that world of sun-drenched perfection.

We all know what happened next. The festival was a catastrophic failure. The private island was a barren construction site. The luxury villas were disaster-relief tents. The gourmet food was a slice of cheese on untoasted bread served in a foam container. The entire enterprise was a fraud, a Potemkin village built of Instagram posts and wishful thinking. The attendees, who had arrived expecting paradise, found themselves in a nightmare, stranded with no food, no water, and no way home. The story of Fyre Festival is a modern parable, a cautionary tale about the power of manufactured desire. But it is also a perfect illustration of the final, and perhaps most profound, of the Ten Commandments: "You shall not covet."

This commandment is different from the nine that precede it. The others are about actions. Do not murder. Do not steal. Do not commit adultery. They are, for the most part, about what you do with your hands, your body, your words. But the Tenth Commandment is about what happens in your heart, in the secret, silent theatre of your mind. It is a commandment about desire itself. It is a law against a feeling. And in a world saturated with images of what we don't have, it may be the most counter-cultural and psychologically astute of them all.

To understand why, we need to journey into the very wiring of the human brain, into the ancient neural circuits that govern our deepest motivations. We need to understand the strange, often paradoxical, relationship between wanting and liking, and how our modern world has systematically hijacked the former at the expense of the latter.

The Wanting Machine: Dopamine and the Endless Loop

For decades, scientists believed that dopamine, a neurotransmitter famous for its role in the brain's reward system, was the "pleasure chemical." The story was simple: do something that feels good—eat a piece of chocolate, have sex, win a game—and your brain releases dopamine, making you feel happy and reinforcing the behaviour. It was a neat, tidy explanation. And it was wrong.

The truth, as pioneering research by neuroscientist Kent Berridge and his colleagues has shown, is far more subtle and, for our purposes, far more important. Berridge's work has revealed that the brain's reward system is not a single, monolithic entity. It is composed of at least two distinct, dissociable systems: a "liking" system and a "wanting" system.

The "liking" system is responsible for the actual experience of pleasure. It is mediated primarily by the brain's opioid system, the same system targeted by drugs like heroin and morphine. When you savour a delicious meal or enjoy a beautiful sunset, it is your "liking" system that is active. It is the feeling of satisfaction, of contentment, of hedonic enjoyment.

The "wanting" system, on the other hand, is driven by dopamine. Its job is not to produce pleasure, but to motivate you to seek it. It is the engine of desire, the neural circuitry of craving. It is what makes you get up off the couch and go to the fridge. It is what makes you swipe right on a dating app. It is what makes you click "buy now" on a product you just saw advertised. Berridge calls this system "incentive salience." It is what makes certain things in the environment stand out, grab your attention, and become motivationally attractive. It transforms a neutral stimulus into a desired goal.

Ordinarily, these two systems work in harmony. You want what you like, and you like what you want. But they can be separated. And when they are, the results are deeply revealing. In a series of now-famous experiments, Berridge and his team were able to activate the dopamine-driven "wanting" system in rats independently of the "liking" system. The results were astonishing. The rats became "super-wanters." They would work frantically to obtain a sugar pellet, pressing a lever hundreds of times, even when they were already full. But when they actually received the sugar, they showed no more signs of "liking" it than a normal rat. Their facial expressions, the rat equivalent of a smile, were no different. They wanted it, but they didn't enjoy it.

This is the dopamine paradox: "wanting" can exist without "liking." And this, in a nutshell, is the neurobiological basis of coveting. Coveting is the state of being trapped in the "wanting" loop. It is a state of perpetual, unfulfilled desire, a craving for something that, even if obtained, may not bring the satisfaction we expect. Our modern world, with its relentless stream of advertising, its curated social media feeds, and its culture of consumerism, is a giant, dopamine-hacking machine. It is designed to keep us in a state of "wanting," to constantly present us with new objects of desire, to make us feel that what we have is not enough.

The Comparison Engine: How Social Media Fuels Envy

If the dopamine system is the engine of coveting, then social comparison is the fuel. In 1954, the social psychologist Leon Festinger proposed his now-famous social comparison theory. His central idea was simple: humans have a fundamental drive to evaluate their own opinions and abilities. And in the absence of objective, non-social standards, we do this by comparing ourselves to others.

This is not, in itself, a bad thing. Social comparison can be a powerful tool for self-improvement. By comparing ourselves to someone who is better at a skill we want to learn, we can be motivated to practice and improve. This is called "upward social comparison." But it has a dark side. When the comparison is not about a specific skill, but about a general state of being—happiness, wealth, attractiveness, success—upward social comparison can be a recipe for misery. It can trigger feelings of envy, inadequacy, and low self-esteem.

For most of human history, our social comparison pool was limited. We compared ourselves to our neighbours, our co-workers, the people in our village. But the advent of social media has changed everything. Suddenly, our comparison pool is global. We are no longer comparing ourselves to the Joneses next door; we are comparing ourselves to the Kardashians, to the billionaire tech entrepreneurs, to the supermodels on private jets. We are comparing our messy, complicated, behind-the-scenes reality to everyone else's perfectly curated, filtered, and edited highlight reel.

The result is a pandemic of envy. A 2020 study by Jin Kyun Lee found that a higher social comparison orientation on social networking sites was directly linked to lower psychological well-being. The constant exposure to idealised images of others' lives leads to a chronic sense of dissatisfaction with our own. We see our friend's perfect holiday photos, and our own recent trip feels inadequate. We see a colleague's promotion announcement, and our own career feels stalled. We see a celebrity's flawless body, and our own reflection in the mirror becomes a source of shame.

This is the mathematical impossibility of happiness in an age of envy. If our happiness is contingent on having what others have, we are doomed to fail. There will always be someone who is richer, more successful, more attractive, more popular. The goalposts are always moving. The game is rigged. As the philosopher Søren Kierkegaard wrote, "Envy is a kind of admiration in disguise." But it is a poisonous admiration, one that corrodes the soul and makes genuine happiness impossible.

The Hedonic Treadmill: The Futility of Acquisition

But what if we do succeed? What if we finally get the thing we have been coveting—the new car, the bigger house, the promotion, the perfect partner? Surely then we will be happy. The research on this question is sobering. In a landmark 1978 study, Philip Brickman and his colleagues studied two groups of people who had experienced major life events: lottery winners and victims of catastrophic accidents that had left them paralysed. The lottery winners, as expected, reported a huge spike in happiness immediately after their win. The accident victims reported a devastating drop. But when the researchers followed up with them months later, they found something remarkable. Both groups had largely returned to their previous baseline levels of happiness. The lottery winners were not significantly happier than they had been before their win. And the accident victims, while still facing immense challenges, were not as unhappy as one might expect. They had, for the most part, adapted.

This phenomenon is known as "hedonic adaptation," or the "hedonic treadmill." It is the human tendency to quickly return to a relatively stable level of happiness despite major positive or negative life events. We are, in a sense, on a treadmill. We can run as fast as we want, but we stay in the same place. The thrill of a new purchase, the joy of a new achievement, the excitement of a new relationship—it all fades. We adapt. We get used to it. And then we start looking for the next thing to make us happy.

This is the final piece of the puzzle of coveting. It is a triple-bind. First, the dopamine-driven "wanting" system keeps us in a perpetual state of desire, often for things we don't even "like." Second, the social comparison engine of modern media ensures that there is always something new to want, something that someone else has that we don't. And third, the hedonic treadmill ensures that even if we get what we want, it won't make us happy for long. It is a recipe for a life of quiet desperation, a life spent chasing a horizon that is always receding.

The Modern Pathology of Desire

This triple-bind has created a modern pathology of desire, a set of cultural sicknesses that are rooted in the sin of coveting. We see it in the phenomenon of **consumer**

dissatisfaction. The average Western consumer is bombarded with thousands of advertisements every day, each one a carefully crafted message designed to create a sense of lack. Your car is too old. Your phone is too slow. Your clothes are out of fashion. Your life is incomplete. The solution, of course, is to buy something. But as the hedonic treadmill teaches us, the satisfaction is fleeting. The new car becomes just "the car." The new phone becomes just "the phone." And the cycle begins again. This is the engine of modern capitalism, a system that depends on the perpetual creation of new desires.

We see it in the rise of **chronic anxiety**. When our sense of self-worth is tied to what we have, we are in a constant state of insecurity. There is always the fear of losing what we have, and the anxiety of not being able to get what we want. This is particularly acute in the realm of social media, where the currency is not money, but likes, followers, and shares. The pressure to present a perfect life, to keep up with the latest trends, to be constantly "on," is a recipe for burnout and anxiety. The fear of missing out (FOMO), a direct product of social comparison, becomes a constant, low-grade hum in the background of our lives.

And we see it in the erosion of **social trust**. A society that is built on coveting is a society that is built on competition. It is a zero-sum game, where your gain is my loss. This breeds resentment, suspicion, and hostility. It undermines the very foundations of community, which are built on cooperation, mutual support, and a shared sense of the common good. When we see our neighbour not as a fellow traveller, but as a rival, the bonds of trust that hold society together begin to fray.

The Social Consequences of Envy

Beyond the personal toll of anxiety and dissatisfaction, a society organised around coveting is a society tearing itself apart. When envy becomes a dominant cultural force, it doesn't just make individuals unhappy; it corrodes the very fabric of social life. It fuels political polarisation, erodes trust in institutions, and can even pave the way for violence.

Consider the political realm. Much of modern political rhetoric is an exercise in weaponised envy. It is the art of convincing one group of people that their problems are the fault of another group, who have unfairly taken what is rightfully theirs. The populist leader tells the working-class man that his job was stolen by an immigrant. The progressive activist tells the young person that their lack of wealth is the fault of the greedy one percent. The talk-radio host tells his listeners that their cultural values are being destroyed by coastal elites. In every case, the emotional logic is the same: someone else has what you deserve, and you should be angry about it. This is not a call for justice, which is about restoring a moral order. It is a call for resentment, which is about punishing those who have more.

A society marinated in this kind of rhetoric becomes a landscape of warring tribes, each defined by its grievances. We cease to see each other as fellow citizens engaged in a common project. We see each other as rivals in a zero-sum game. Political discourse is no longer about persuasion and compromise; it is about vanquishing the enemy. The goal is not to build a more perfect union, but to take back what is ours.

This culture of envy also has a devastating effect on our institutions. When we believe that the system is rigged, that success is always the result of cheating or privilege, we lose faith in the very idea of a meritocratic society. We become cynical about the possibility of genuine achievement. The successful entrepreneur is not admired for their innovation and hard work, but suspected of exploitation. The respected professional is not seen as a model of expertise, but as a gatekeeper of an unjust system. This cynicism is corrosive. It eats away at the trust that is essential for a functioning economy and a stable democracy. If we believe that everyone is just out for themselves, that no one can be trusted, then the only rational response is to be out for ourselves as well. The social contract is dissolved.

At its most extreme, envy can be a justification for violence. The history of the 20th century is littered with examples of totalitarian regimes that rose to power by harnessing the politics of resentment. The kulaks in the Soviet Union, the bourgeoisie in China, the Jews in Nazi Germany—in each case, a group was identified as the source of the nation's problems, their success was framed as a form of theft, and their persecution and eventual extermination was presented as an act of social justice. This is the terrifying endpoint of a culture of coveting. It is a path that begins with a resentful glance at a neighbour's new car and can end in a concentration camp.

This is why the Tenth Commandment is so critical. It is not just a piece of personal moral advice. It is a foundational principle of a free and humane society. It is a recognition that a society that celebrates envy is a society that is on the road to ruin.

Coveting as Misdirected Worship

At its deepest level, the Tenth Commandment reveals that coveting is not just a psychological problem; it is a spiritual one. It is a form of misdirected worship. As we saw in Chapter 1, we are all worshippers. We are all oriented around some ultimate value, some "god" that gives our lives meaning and purpose. The first commandment, "You shall have no other gods before me," establishes the proper object of our worship. The Tenth Commandment shows us what happens when we get it wrong.

When we covet, we are essentially saying that our neighbour's possessions, or our neighbour's life, is our god. We are looking to something created to give us the security, the identity, and the happiness that can only be found in the Creator. We are bowing down to the idol of "more." This is why the Apostle Paul, in his letter to the Colossians, calls greed a form of idolatry. It is the worship of the self, and the self's insatiable desires.

This is the ultimate dead end of coveting. It promises happiness, but it delivers anxiety. It promises fulfillment, but it delivers emptiness. It promises life, but it delivers a kind of living death, a state of being perpetually haunted by what we are not. It is, as the writer Joseph Epstein once put it, "the one sin that has no fun in it."

The Christian Vision: The Freedom of Contentment

It is into this psychological and spiritual maelstrom that the Tenth Commandment speaks its radical, liberating word: "You shall not covet." This is not, as it is often misunderstood, a prohibition against all desire. Desire is a fundamental part of being human. It is the engine of creativity, of ambition, of love. The Bible is full of exhortations to desire good things: to desire wisdom, to desire justice, to desire God himself. The problem is not desire, but disordered desire. The problem is coveting.

To covet is to desire what is not rightfully yours, what belongs to your neighbour. It is to see your neighbour's life—their house, their spouse, their job, their success—not as a source of joy or inspiration, but as a source of pain, as a reminder of what you lack. It is to live in a state of perpetual comparison, to see the world not as a gift to be received with gratitude, but as a zero-sum game to be won.

The Christian tradition offers a radical alternative to this way of life: the virtue of contentment. Contentment is not resignation. It is not a passive acceptance of a miserable lot in life. It is, rather, a deep, abiding trust that what we have is enough, because the one who has given it to us is enough. It is the freedom that comes from anchoring our identity not in what we possess, but in who we are as beloved children of God.

The Apostle Paul, writing from a Roman prison, put it this way: "I have learned to be content whatever the circumstances. I know what it is to be in need, and I know what it is to have plenty. I have learned the secret of being content in any and every situation, whether well fed or hungry, whether living in plenty or in want. I can do all this through him who gives me strength."

This is a stunning statement. Paul is not saying that his circumstances don't matter. He is saying that his contentment is not dependent on them. His joy is not a fragile, fleeting thing, subject to the whims of fortune. It is a deep, resilient, and abiding peace, rooted in his relationship with Christ. He has stepped off the hedonic treadmill. He has escaped the "wanting" loop. He has found the secret of being content.

The Path Forward: Cultivating a Contented Heart

How, then, can we cultivate this kind of contentment in our own lives? How can we resist the siren song of coveting in a world that is constantly telling us to want more? The Christian tradition offers a set of practices, a kind of spiritual physiotherapy for the desiring heart.

First, there is the practice of **gratitude**. This is more than just a fleeting feeling; it is a cultivated discipline. It is the active, intentional choice to focus on what we have, rather than what we lack. It is a way of retraining our attention, of consciously redirecting our gaze from the curated highlight reels of others to the small, often overlooked gifts of our own lives. This could be as simple as keeping a gratitude journal, where you write down three things you are thankful for each day. It could be the practice of "gratitude walks," where you intentionally look for things in your environment to be thankful for. It could be the habit of expressing your gratitude to others, of writing a letter to someone who has made a difference in your life. These practices, as research by psychologists like Robert Emmons has shown, have a powerful effect on our well-being. They increase our sense of happiness, reduce feelings of envy and resentment, and even improve our physical health. Gratitude is a powerful antidote to the poison of envy because it changes the fundamental question we are asking. Instead of asking, "What do I lack?", we begin to ask, "What have I been given?"

Second, there is the practice of **generosity**. Coveting is a form of hoarding, a desperate, clenched-fist attempt to accumulate more for ourselves. Generosity is its opposite. It is the open-handed, joyful act of giving away what we have for the good of others. This is not just about writing a cheque to a charity. It is about a posture of the heart, a willingness to share our time, our talents, and our resources with those in need. It could mean volunteering at a local food bank, mentoring a young person, or simply buying a coffee for the person behind you in line. Generosity breaks the logic of the zero-sum game. It is a powerful declaration that the world is not a place of scarcity, but of abundance. It reminds us that we are not just consumers, but conduits of God's grace. And paradoxically, it is in giving that we receive. Research on the "helper's high" has shown that acts of altruism trigger the release of endorphins in the brain, creating a sense of well-being and connection. Generosity is a declaration that our security does not lie in what we possess, but in the one who possesses us.

Third, there is the practice of **Sabbath**. As we saw in Chapter 4, the Sabbath is a weekly act of resistance against the culture of endless productivity and consumption. It is a day for delighting in the world as it is, not as we want it to be. It is a day for enjoying the simple, non-commodified pleasures of life: a walk in the park, a meal with friends, a good book. It is a day for remembering that our value does not come from what we produce or what we own, but from the simple fact that we are made in the image of God.

Finally, there is the practice of **worship**. This is the ultimate reordering of our desires. To worship God is to declare that he, and not our possessions, not our status, not our achievements, is the ultimate source of our joy. It is to find our deepest satisfaction not in the created world, but in the Creator. It is to say with the psalmist, "Whom have I in heaven but you? And earth has nothing I desire besides you. My flesh and my heart may fail, but God is the strength of my heart and my portion forever."

The Test: Are You Living by the Law of Contentment?

How can you know if you are living by the Law of Contentment? Here are a few diagnostic questions to consider:

- **How do you react to the success of others?** When a friend or colleague shares good news, is your first reaction genuine joy for them, or a pang of envy? Do you find yourself secretly hoping for them to fail, just a little, so that you don't feel so bad about your own life?

- **How much time do you spend on social media?** And how do you feel after you have been scrolling? Do you feel inspired and connected, or drained and dissatisfied? Are you using it to build genuine community, or to fuel a cycle of comparison and envy?

- **What is your relationship with money and possessions?** Do you see them as tools to be used for the glory of God and the good of others, or as a source of security and identity? Are you able to give generously, or do you find yourself hoarding what you have out of fear?

- **Where do you find your deepest sense of self-worth?** Is it in your job title, your bank account, your physical appearance, your social status? Or is it in the unshakeable, unconditional love of God?

These are not easy questions. They require a level of honesty and self-awareness that can be uncomfortable. But they are essential if we are to break free from the tyranny of coveting and enter into the freedom of contentment.

Conclusion: The End of the Law

And so we come to the end of our journey through the Ten Commandments. We have seen how these ancient laws, far from being a set of arbitrary rules, are a profound and practical guide to human flourishing. They are a description of the very architecture of reality, a user's manual for the human soul. They show us how to live in right relationship with God, with our neighbour, and with ourselves.

They begin with the ultimate reality: the one true God who is the source of all being and the proper object of our worship. They move to the proper way to represent and speak of this God, with reverence and awe. They establish a rhythm of work and rest that is essential for our physical and mental health. They lay the foundation for a stable society by protecting the bonds of family, the sanctity of life, the integrity of marriage, the right to property, and the necessity of truth. And they end here, with this final, inward-looking commandment, a call to find our contentment not in the endless pursuit of more, but in the joyful acceptance of enough.

In a world that is increasingly fragmented, anxious, and polarised, these ancient laws offer a path to wholeness, to peace, and to a life of deep and lasting joy. They are not a burden, but a gift. They are not a cage, but a key. They are, as the Apostle Paul wrote, "holy, righteous, and good." And they point us, ultimately, to the one who is the fulfillment of the law, the one in whom all our deepest desires find their true and lasting home.

This is the great secret of the Ten Commandments. They are not, in the end, about what we must do to earn God's favour. They are a description of what life looks like when we have already received it. They are the shape of freedom. They are the grammar of love. And in a world that has lost its way, they are a map that can lead us home.

CHAPTER 11: Why These Laws Work (Even If You Don't Believe in God)

In the early 2000s, a team of anthropologists and computer scientists at the Santa Fe Institute, a think tank in the high desert of New Mexico, embarked on a curious project. They were building a simulated world, a digital society they called 'Artificial Anasazi.' Their goal was to understand the mysterious disappearance of the Anasazi people from the Four Corners region of the United States in the late 13th century. For decades, archaeologists had debated the cause of the collapse. Was it drought? Warfare? Disease? The researchers at Santa Fe wanted to see if they could replicate the society's rise and fall using computer models.

They programmed their digital 'agents' with a few basic rules drawn from what we know about human behaviour and the archaeological record. The agents needed to find food and water. They formed households. They had a limited lifespan. And, crucially, they made decisions based on the success of their neighbours. If a household in a nearby valley was thriving, other agents were more likely to move there. It was a simple, elegant model, a world in miniature. As the simulation ran, something remarkable happened. The digital society grew, expanded, and built settlements in patterns that uncannily mirrored the real archaeological sites scattered across the mesas and canyons of the Southwest. Then, as the virtual environment experienced simulated droughts, the society began to unravel. The agents abandoned their homes, the population plummeted, and the once-thriving settlements became ghost towns. The simulation had, with startling accuracy, reproduced a centuries-old mystery [1].

What the Artificial Anasazi project demonstrated was a profound truth about human societies: complex outcomes can emerge from very simple rules. You don't need to program every individual with a grand, top-down plan. You just need to give them a few fundamental principles to follow, and a coherent, functioning society will emerge. The simulation was, in its own way, a testament to the power of what we might call 'compression algorithms' for social order—simple, elegant rules that, when followed, produce stable, predictable, and flourishing communities.

For the past ten chapters, we have been on a journey through what might be the most famous set of compression algorithms ever devised: the Ten Commandments. We have explored them not as a list of arbitrary prohibitions from a distant, ancient deity, but as a startlingly sophisticated user's manual for the human soul. We have seen how the Law of Primacy ("You shall have no other gods") describes our non-negotiable need for a stable value hierarchy. We have examined how the Law of Fidelity ("You shall not commit adultery") provides the source code for the trust that makes long-term pair-bonding possible. We have unpacked the psychological necessity of rest, the cognitive poison of envy, and the social corrosion of lies. In each case, we have found that these ancient laws map, with uncanny precision, onto the deepest structures of our psychology, our biology, and our social dynamics.

But now we arrive at the most crucial question of all. *Why?* Why do these particular laws work? Why do they possess this enduring power, this seeming universality that transcends time, culture, and even belief? If you don't believe they were handed down on tablets of stone from a burning mountain, how do you account for their extraordinary resilience? Is it mere coincidence that the principles they embody seem to be rediscovered, in different forms, by cultures all over the world? Or is something deeper going on?

This chapter is an attempt to answer that question. It is a synthesis of what we have learned, an exploration of the underlying mechanics of this ancient moral technology. We will argue that the Ten Commandments are not arbitrary. They are, in effect, a description of reality. They are a set of psychological and social axioms that have been discovered, forgotten, and rediscovered throughout human history because they are woven into the very fabric of our being. They are the instruction manual that came with the machine. You can, of course, choose to reject the Manufacturer, but you cannot, it seems, escape the design of the machine itself.

The Universal Moral Code

In 2019, a team of anthropologists at the University of Oxford, led by Dr. Oliver Scott Curry, published the results of a groundbreaking study. They had conducted the largest and most comprehensive cross-cultural survey of morals ever attempted, analysing ethnographic data from 60 different societies around the globe, from the Amhara of Ethiopia to the Garo of India and the Maasai of Kenya. Their goal was to test a theory known as 'morality-as-cooperation,' which predicts that if morality evolved to promote cooperation, then the specific moral rules found in different cultures should all be variations on this central theme. They wanted to know if humanity, in all its sprawling, diverse glory, shared a common moral code [2].

What they found was a stunning confirmation of the theory. Across all 60 cultures, they identified seven moral rules that were always considered good, always seen as the right way to behave:

- Help your family.
- Help your group.
- Return favours.
- Be brave.
- Defer to superiors.
- Divide resources fairly.
- Respect others' property.

As Dr. Curry explained, "Everyone everywhere shares a common moral code. All agree that cooperating, promoting the common good, is the right thing to do" [2]. The specific applications of these rules might vary, but the underlying principles were universal. The Maasai admired warrior virtues because bravery helped protect the group. The Korean 'egalitarian community ethic' of mutual assistance strengthened in-group solidarity. The Garo of India placed a high value on reciprocity because returning favours is the bedrock of social exchange. Crucially, the researchers found no counter-examples. No society on Earth believed that helping your family was bad, that respecting property was wrong, or that fairness was immoral.

What is so striking about this list is how closely it mirrors the principles encoded in the Ten Commandments. "Help your family" is a secular echo of "Honour your father and your mother." "Respect others' property" is the core of "You shall not steal." The prohibitions against bearing false witness and coveting are designed to protect the very foundations of fairness and reciprocity that allow a group to function. The commandments against murder and adultery are, at their heart, about creating the safety and stability necessary for a group to survive and thrive. The Oxford study, using the rigorous methods of modern anthropology, had essentially rediscovered the core tenets of the Decalogue, not as divine revelation, but as the observable, practical wisdom of our species.

This is the first key to understanding why these laws work. They are not the arbitrary invention of one culture or one religion. This sacred operating system was given to us by God, and since then, we keep rediscovering the same things: they are the product of a global, multi-generational discovery process. They are the solutions that human beings, again and again, have stumbled upon to solve the fundamental problems of living together. How do we create trust? How do we care for the next generation? How do we resolve disputes without violence? How do we build a society that is more than just a collection of self-interested individuals? God could have just said, 'I told you so.'

The Ten Commandments are a compression algorithm for the answers to these questions. They are a distillation of thousands of years of human experience, a set of heuristics for flourishing. God revealed them because they work. They work because they are aligned with the deep logic of cooperation that has allowed our species to build everything from small hunter-gatherer bands to sprawling global civilisations.

The Brain's Moral Compass

But the explanation cannot stop there. It is not enough to say that these rules promote cooperation. We must also ask *how* they do so. What is it about our minds, our brains, that makes these particular rules so effective? The answer, it turns out, lies in the very architecture of our neural hardware.

Consider the strange and tragic case of Phineas Gage. In 1848, Gage was a railway foreman in Vermont, a man known for his competence, his reliability, and his good character. One afternoon, an accidental explosion sent a three-foot-long iron rod hurtling through his skull, entering under his left cheekbone and exiting through the top of his head. Miraculously, Gage survived. He could walk, talk, and remember. But he was no longer Gage. His personality had been utterly transformed. The once-responsible foreman was now impulsive, profane, and incapable of holding down a job or maintaining relationships. His friends said he was "no longer Gage."

For over a century, Gage's case was a medical curiosity. But with the advent of modern neuroscience, researchers were able to reconstruct the path of the iron rod and identify the precise area of his brain that had been destroyed: the ventromedial prefrontal cortex (vmPFC). This region, located just behind the forehead, has since been identified as a critical hub in the brain's moral decision-making network [3]. It is not the brain's 'moral centre,' but it acts as a kind of switchboard, integrating the emotional signals from deeper, more ancient parts of the brain, like the amygdala (which processes fear and empathy), with the more rational, deliberative functions of the dorsolateral prefrontal cortex. The vmPFC is what allows us to attach emotional weight to our decisions, to feel the wrongness of an action, not just to calculate its consequences.

When this region is damaged, as it was in Gage, the result is a kind of 'acquired sociopathy.' Patients with vmPFC lesions can often reason about moral dilemmas in a purely abstract, utilitarian way. They know the rules, but the rules have no emotional force for them. They will say that it is permissible to push a large man off a bridge to stop a runaway trolley from killing five people, a choice that most neurologically typical people find deeply abhorrent, because the cold logic of saving five lives outweighs the visceral, emotional horror of killing one. They have lost the gut feeling that makes morality more than just a logical puzzle [4].

What the neuroscience of morality reveals is that the Ten Commandments are not just abstract ethical principles; they are deeply resonant with the way our brains are wired. The prohibitions against murder, theft, and betrayal are not simply good ideas; they are rules that tap into the most fundamental emotional and social circuits in our minds.

"You shall not murder" is not just a social contract; it is a command that resonates with the amygdala's powerful, visceral response to the sight of harm and distress in others. When we witness violence, our mirror neurones fire in sympathy. Our heart rate increases. We feel the other person's pain as if it were our own. This is not a learned response; it is wired into us at the deepest level. The prohibition against murder is, in a sense, simply a formalisation of what our brains are already screaming at us: that the suffering of another human being is intolerable.

"You shall not commit adultery" is not just a rule about sexual fidelity; it is a principle that protects the deep, oxytocin-fuelled bonds of attachment that form the basis of our most intimate relationships and the stability of our families. When we form a pair bond with another person, our brains undergo a remarkable transformation. The reward circuits that light up when we see our partner are the same circuits that light up when we see our children. We are neurologically bonded to them. Betrayal of that bond is, quite literally, a violation of the brain's deepest attachment systems, and the damage it causes is profound and long-lasting.

"You shall not bear false witness" is not just a legal requirement; it is a recognition that our brains are exquisitely tuned to detect deception and that trust, the glue of all social life, is impossible without a shared commitment to the truth. We are lie-detection machines. We read faces, tone of voice, body language. We are constantly assessing whether the people around us are being honest with us. When we discover that someone has lied to us, particularly someone we trusted, the betrayal triggers a cascade of negative emotions: anger, hurt, shame, and a fundamental loss of faith in our ability to navigate the social world.

When we violate these rules, we are not just breaking a social convention; we are acting against the grain of our own neurobiology. We are creating a cognitive and emotional dissonance that is deeply unsettling. The guilt, the shame, the anxiety that follow from immoral actions are not just social constructs; they are the brain's alarm system, signalling that we have gone off-course, that we have damaged the very relationships and structures that we depend on for our survival and well-being.

This is why rejecting the laws doesn't remove their consequences. You can decide that the prohibition against stealing is an outdated social construct, but your nervous system will still register the stress of potential discovery, the guilt of taking what is not yours, and the social isolation that comes from being known as untrustworthy. You can dismiss the law of fidelity as an oppressive relic, but you cannot escape the psychological devastation that betrayal inflicts on the human attachment system. As we saw in Chapter 7, betrayal trauma is not just a broken heart; it is a profound violation of our sense of safety and reality, one that can lead to long-term psychological damage, including anxiety, depression, and post-traumatic stress [5]. The laws work because they are a user's manual for a machine that is already built in a particular way.

The Unseen Costs of Rejection: Case Studies in Social Collapse

This brings us to the final, and perhaps most confronting, piece of the puzzle. If these laws are so deeply embedded in our nature, if they are the product of a universal human wisdom, and if they are aligned with the very structure of our brains, what happens when a society decides to reject them?

We are, in many ways, living through a global experiment designed to answer that very question. For the past several decades, Western culture has been engaged in a project of systematic deconstruction, attempting to liberate the individual from the perceived constraints of these ancient moral frameworks. We have been told that happiness lies in radical autonomy, in the casting off of unchosen obligations, and in the pursuit of self-defined truths. The results of this experiment are now coming in, and they are not encouraging.

The Trust Collapse

As we discussed in Chapter 9, the decline of a shared commitment to truth has led to a crisis of social trust. A 2025 article in *Psychology Today* highlighted the staggering erosion of trust in modern life. In the 1950s, roughly three-quarters of Americans believed the government would do the right thing most of the time, and 60 percent trusted their neighbours. Today, those numbers have plummeted to less than a quarter and a third, respectively [6]. We live in an age of pervasive suspicion, where we are increasingly isolated from one another, cocooned in digital echo chambers that amplify our biases and reinforce our distrust of those who are different.

The mechanism behind this collapse is worth examining in detail. Technology, which promised to connect us, has done the opposite. When we communicate face-to-face, our brains are flooded with information: the warmth of a smile, the sincerity in someone's eyes, the genuine concern in their voice. These cues are processed automatically by our amygdala and our mirror neurone system, creating a sense of safety and connection. But digital communication strips away these cues. A delayed text message, a dry email, a message left on read—these ambiguous signals are interpreted by our threat-detection systems as signs of rejection or hostility. Over time, this creates a state of chronic vigilance, a low-level anxiety that pervades our relationships [6].

The algorithms that govern social media have made this worse. They are designed to maximise engagement, and engagement is maximised by outrage. Content that makes us angry, that confirms our suspicions about others, that portrays people who disagree with us as not just wrong but evil—this is what the algorithms promote. We are literally being fed a diet of content designed to make us distrust one another. And it is working. Studies show that increased social media use is associated with higher levels of loneliness and lower levels of trust [6].

The Loneliness Epidemic

This collapse of trust has had devastating psychological consequences. Loneliness has become a public health epidemic, with studies showing that it is as damaging to our physical health as smoking 15 cigarettes a day [7]. Rates of anxiety and depression have skyrocketed, particularly among young people. We have more freedom, more wealth, and more technological power than any generation in history, and yet we are more miserable.

The United States Surgeon General has declared loneliness a public health crisis. In the United Kingdom, the government appointed a "Minister for Loneliness" to address the problem. In Japan, there is a phenomenon called *kodokushi*—"lonely death"—where elderly people die alone in their homes and are not discovered for weeks or months. These are not isolated incidents; they are symptoms of a systemic breakdown in the social fabric.

What is particularly striking is that loneliness is not correlated with living alone. Some of the loneliest people are those surrounded by others, scrolling through social media, watching other people's curated highlight reels of happiness and connection. They are, in a very real sense, experiencing what the psychologist Sherry Turkle calls "alone together"—physically proximate but emotionally isolated. The problem is not the absence of people; it is the absence of genuine connection, of the kind of deep, embodied, face-to-face intimacy that our brains are wired for.

The Breakdown of Institutions

The erosion of trust has also had profound consequences for our institutions. When people no longer believe that their government, their media, their doctors, or their teachers are acting in good faith, the entire social order becomes unstable. We have seen this play out in real time over the past decade. Conspiracy theories flourish. Vaccination rates decline. Political polarisation intensifies. The shared reality that holds a society together begins to fracture.

Consider the case of the COVID-19 pandemic. In countries with high levels of social trust, like Denmark and South Korea, the pandemic response was relatively coordinated and effective. People trusted their government's guidance, complied with public health measures, and the virus was brought under control relatively quickly. But in countries with lower levels of trust, like the United States and the United Kingdom, the response was chaotic and fragmented. People didn't trust the government, so they didn't follow the guidelines. They didn't trust the vaccines, so they didn't get vaccinated. The result was higher death rates, longer lockdowns, and greater economic damage.

This is not a coincidence. Trust is the operating system of society. When it breaks down, everything else breaks down with it. And the breakdown of trust is directly traceable to the violation of the commandment against bearing false witness. When institutions lie to the public, when politicians mislead, when media outlets present propaganda as news, they are poisoning the well from which all social cooperation flows.

The consequences are visible everywhere. In education, students no longer trust that their teachers have their best interests at heart. In medicine, patients question whether doctors are recommending treatments based on evidence or profit. In law enforcement, communities view the police not as protectors but as oppressors. In business, consumers assume that corporations are trying to deceive them. Each of these breakdowns of trust makes the institution less effective. Teachers who are not trusted cannot teach effectively. Doctors who are not trusted cannot heal. Police who are not trusted cannot maintain order. The institution becomes a hollow shell, going through the motions but lacking the moral authority that makes it function.

What is particularly insidious is that once trust is lost, it is extraordinarily difficult to regain. Trust is built slowly, through thousands of small acts of integrity and honesty. But it can be destroyed in an instant by a single act of deception. And once destroyed, the assumption shifts. Instead of assuming good faith, people assume bad faith. They interpret ambiguous actions in the worst possible light. They assume that institutions are lying, even when they are telling the truth. This is what psychologists call "negative sentiment override," and it is corrosive to the social fabric.

The Meaning Crisis

Perhaps most troubling is what we might call the "meaning crisis." In our attempt to liberate ourselves from the constraints of traditional morality, we have also liberated ourselves from the frameworks that give life meaning. We are told that we are free to define our own values, to create our own meaning. But the result, for many people, is a profound sense of emptiness and purposelessness.

The psychologist Viktor Frankl, who survived the Nazi concentration camps, argued that the primary human motivation is not pleasure or power, but the search for meaning. When we lose a sense of meaning, we become vulnerable to despair, to addiction, to nihilism. And this is precisely what we are seeing in modern Western societies. Rates of substance abuse have skyrocketed. Suicide rates have increased, particularly among middle-aged men and teenagers. Mental health crises are epidemic.

Consider the opioid crisis that has devastated communities across North America. Hundreds of thousands of people have died from overdoses, and millions more are struggling with addiction. The conventional explanation focuses on pharmaceutical companies, on the over-prescription of painkillers, on the lack of treatment facilities. All of these factors are real and important. But there is a deeper issue at work. Many of the people who became addicted to opioids were living in communities that had lost their economic purpose. Factories had closed. Jobs had disappeared. The meaning that work had provided—the sense of being part of something, of contributing to the community, of having a role to play—had evaporated. In the absence of that meaning, people turned to drugs. The opioid was not just a physical escape from pain; it was an existential escape from meaninglessness.

Similarly, the rising rates of suicide among middle-aged men in wealthy countries cannot be explained by poverty or lack of access to material goods. These men have money, they have homes, they have the material trappings of success. But they have lost the sense of purpose that gave their lives meaning. They were told that their role was to be breadwinners, to provide for their families. But in a world where that role is no longer valued, where they are told that their contribution is not needed, they are left adrift. Without a sense of purpose, life becomes unbearable.

The irony is that the Ten Commandments, far from being a constraint on meaning, are actually a source of it. They provide a framework for understanding our place in the world, our obligations to others, and our ultimate purpose. They tell us that our lives matter, that our choices have consequences, that we are part of something larger than ourselves. They tell us that we have a duty to care for our families, to contribute to our communities, to be honest and fair in our dealings with others. These are not burdensome constraints; they are invitations to a meaningful life. In rejecting them, we have not become freer; we have become adrift.

SIDE NOTE: A Hypothetical Paradise

To understand the full power of the Ten Commandments, it is useful to imagine what a society would look like if it achieved perfect adherence to them. This is not a realistic scenario—human beings are fallible, and perfect obedience to any moral code is impossible. But as a thought experiment, it is illuminating.

The Foundation: Primacy and Transcendence

In our hypothetical society, every individual has a clear, stable hierarchy of values. At the apex of this hierarchy sits something transcendent—whether that is God, truth, beauty, or the common good. This is not a tyranny imposed from above, but a freely chosen orientation that gives coherence and direction to each person's life. As a result, people are not constantly buffeted by conflicting desires and impulses. They have a sense of purpose. They know what they are working towards.

Because of this clarity of values, the society is not torn apart by ideological conflicts. People disagree about many things, but they are united in their commitment to something larger than themselves. They are not trying to impose their particular vision of the good on everyone else; they are trying to align themselves with a transcendent reality that is accessible to all.

Trust and Fidelity

In this society, the commandment against adultery is observed. Marriages are stable. Children grow up in secure, loving homes where they know they are wanted and valued. The attachment bonds that form in these families are deep and secure. As a result, people grow up with a fundamental sense of safety and trust. They are not hypervigilant or defensive. They can afford to be vulnerable with others because they have learned that vulnerability is safe.

This trust extends beyond the family. Because people have learned to keep their commitments, to be faithful to their promises, the entire social fabric is woven with trust. Contracts are honoured. Promises are kept. People do what they say they will do. As a result, cooperation becomes easy. You don't need elaborate legal systems to enforce agreements, because people are motivated by their own commitment to truth and fidelity.

Justice and Fairness

In this society, the commandments against theft and against coveting are observed. Resources are distributed fairly. People are not consumed by envy or resentment. They are content with their own circumstances and genuinely happy when others prosper. As a result, there is no class warfare, no revolution, no violent conflict over resources. People work hard, not because they are trying to accumulate more than their neighbours, but because they find meaning and satisfaction in their work.

The legal system is minimal, because there is little crime. The police are not militarised; they are community members who are respected and trusted. The courts are fair and impartial. Punishment is designed not for retribution, but for restoration and rehabilitation. Criminals are rare, and when they do occur, they are treated with compassion and a genuine desire to help them reform.

Truth and Community

In this society, the commandment against bearing false witness is observed. People tell the truth. The media reports facts accurately. Politicians are honest about their intentions and their limitations. Scientists publish their findings without fear of censorship or political pressure. As a result, there is a shared reality. People can disagree about values and priorities, but they are working from the same set of facts.

This shared reality creates a sense of community. People understand one another. They can predict how others will behave. They can trust that the information they are receiving is accurate. As a result, public discourse is rational and productive. People listen to one another. They change their minds when presented with good evidence. They work together to solve collective problems.

Rest and Renewal

In this society, the commandment to remember the Sabbath is observed. People work hard during the week, but they take time to rest, to reflect, to spend time with their families and their communities. This rest is not laziness; it is a recognition that human beings need time to recover, to reconnect with what matters most, to step back from the endless treadmill of productivity and consumption.

As a result, people are not burned out. They are not anxious or depressed. They have time to develop their talents, to pursue their passions, to engage in activities that bring them joy and meaning. The culture is not one of endless striving, but of balanced living. People work to live; they don't live to work.

Honour and Continuity

In this society, the commandment to honour your father and mother is observed. Elders are respected. The wisdom of the past is valued. Intergenerational relationships are strong. Young people learn from their elders, and elders find purpose and meaning in passing on their knowledge and experience.

As a result, there is continuity. Society is not constantly reinventing itself, discarding the past and starting anew. Instead, it builds on the foundations laid by previous generations. There is a sense of being part of a long chain of human beings stretching back into the past and forward into the future. This gives people a sense of belonging and purpose that transcends their individual lives.

The Overall Picture

In this hypothetical society, people are not perfect. They still struggle with temptation, with selfishness, with the desire to hurt others. But the commandments provide a framework that makes it easier to do the right thing. The culture supports moral behaviour. The institutions reinforce it. The social norms encourage it.

As a result, people flourish. They are healthy, both physically and mentally. They have meaningful work. They have deep relationships. They have a sense of purpose. They are not anxious about the future, because they trust that the people around them are acting in good faith. They are not lonely, because they are embedded in communities of genuine connection and mutual care.

This is not a utopia. Conflict still exists. Disagreements still arise. But they are resolved through dialogue and compromise, not through violence and coercion. Society is not perfect, but it is fundamentally healthy and stable. It is a place where human beings can flourish.

The Ultimate Paradox

And this, finally, is where the question of God returns, not as a philosophical abstraction, but as a practical necessity. The great insight of the Christian tradition is that these laws are not merely a good idea; they are grounded in the very character of the universe and its Creator. They are not just a human discovery; they are a divine gift. They are an expression of a love that seeks our flourishing, a love that provides the boundaries we need to live in freedom and in peace.

For the believer, the laws work because they come from God. But for the sceptic, the evidence points to a no less astonishing conclusion: the laws work because they describe, with breathtaking accuracy, the world that God has made. You can reject the source, but you cannot escape the structure. The music is written into the score. Whether you believe in the Composer or not, you will find that the only way to play it well is to follow the notes.

The Ten Commandments endure not because they are imposed by force or fear, but because they are aligned with the deepest truths about human nature, human psychology, and human society. They are a map of reality. And in a world that has lost its way, that is perhaps the most radical and revolutionary thing we could possibly discover.

CHAPTER 12: What Happens When a Society Ignores Them

There is a moment in every tragedy when the protagonist realises that their choices have consequences. It comes too late, of course. The damage is already done. But in that moment of recognition, there is a terrible clarity. In the Greek tragedies, this moment is called *anagnorisis*—the recognition. It is the point at which the hero understands, finally, what they have done.

We are living in that moment now. Not as individuals, but as a civilisation. We are beginning to understand, dimly and reluctantly, that the systematic rejection of the moral frameworks that held our societies together has consequences. And those consequences are not abstract or theoretical. They are visible, measurable, and devastating.

This chapter is not about why the laws work. We have already explored that. This chapter is about what happens when they don't. It is about the cascade of failures that occurs when a society decides that the ancient moral wisdom is obsolete, that we have evolved beyond the need for such constraints, that we can build a better world on the rubble of the old one.

The answer is stark: we cannot. And the evidence is all around us.

The Institutional Collapse

In the autumn of 2020, as the world reeled from the shock of the COVID-19 pandemic, something remarkable happened in Denmark. The government announced a lockdown. The people complied. Not because they were forced to, but because they trusted their government. They trusted that the authorities were acting in their best interest, that the information they were receiving was accurate, and that the restrictions, however onerous, were necessary and temporary. The compliance rate was extraordinarily high. The virus was brought under control relatively quickly. Life returned to something approaching normalcy within months.

In the United States, the same period saw a very different story. The government announced restrictions. Significant portions of the population refused to comply. They didn't trust the government. They didn't trust the media. They didn't trust the scientific establishment. Some of this distrust was justified—there were genuine failures of communication and occasional contradictions in the guidance. But much of it was rooted in something deeper: a pervasive belief that institutions were not acting in good faith, that they were pursuing hidden agendas, that they were lying.

The result was catastrophic. Hospitals were overwhelmed. Death rates were higher. The economic damage was greater. The social divisions were deeper. And the trust, already eroded, eroded further. People watched their neighbours die because they refused vaccination based on conspiracy theories. They watched their friends and family members become estranged over political disagreements about public health measures. The pandemic did not create this lack of trust, but it exposed it, and in doing so, it accelerated the collapse.

This is what happens when a society violates the commandment against bearing false witness on a systemic scale. When institutions lie, when politicians mislead, when media outlets present propaganda as news, they are not just breaking a rule. They are poisoning the well from which all cooperation flows. And once that well is poisoned, it is extraordinarily difficult to clean it again.

The consequences ripple outward. In education, students no longer assume that their teachers are acting in their best interest. They assume that teachers are pushing ideological agendas. In medicine, patients question whether doctors are recommending treatments based on evidence or profit. In law enforcement, communities view the police not as protectors but as oppressors. In business, consumers assume that corporations are trying to deceive them. Each of these breakdowns of trust makes the institution less effective. A teacher who is not trusted cannot teach. A doctor who is not trusted cannot heal. A police officer who is not trusted cannot maintain order.

The institution becomes a hollow shell, going through the motions but lacking the moral authority that makes it function. And as the institutions fail, people become increasingly desperate for some source of stability, some authority they can trust. This desperation makes them vulnerable to demagogues, to conspiracy theorists, to anyone who offers a simple explanation for the chaos and a promise of restoration.

Consider the rise of conspiracy theories in recent years. QAnon, anti-vaccination movements, claims that the moon landing was faked, theories about shadowy elites controlling world events—these are not new phenomena. Conspiracy theories have always existed. But they have never been as widespread, as deeply believed, or as consequential as they are now. And the reason is not that people have become more gullible or less intelligent. It is that they have lost trust in the institutions that are supposed to provide them with reliable information.

When the government lies, when the media distorts the truth, when scientists are seen as serving corporate interests rather than the public good, people stop believing anything they are told. They assume that the official narrative is false and that the truth must be hidden. They become susceptible to alternative explanations, no matter how implausible. And once they have committed to a conspiracy theory, the evidence against it only reinforces their belief. They see the debunking as part of the conspiracy.

This is not a problem that can be solved by simply telling people the truth more clearly. The problem is deeper. It is a problem of institutional legitimacy. People will not believe what institutions tell them if they do not trust those institutions. And trust, once lost, is extraordinarily difficult to regain. This is the ultimate cost of violating the commandment against bearing false witness. It is not just that individual lies have consequences. It is that systematic lying destroys the very possibility of a shared reality, a shared set of facts that a society can use to make collective decisions.

The Mental Health Epidemic

In September 2025, the World Health Organisation released a sobering report. More than one billion people are now living with mental health disorders. That is one in every seven human beings on the planet. Anxiety and depression are the most common conditions, affecting people across all ages, income levels, and nations. The economic cost is staggering: depression and anxiety alone cost the global economy an estimated one trillion dollars annually [1].

To put this in perspective, the global economy is approximately one hundred trillion dollars. One percent of that entire output is consumed by depression and anxiety alone. That is not a rounding error. That is not a minor public health issue. That is a civilisational crisis. And the statistics are getting worse. Since the COVID-19 pandemic, rates of depression and anxiety have increased dramatically. Young people are particularly affected. In the United States, the National Institute of Mental Health reports that nearly one in five adults lives with a mental illness. Among adolescents, the rates are even higher. Suicide is the second leading cause of death among young people, after accidents. And the rates have been climbing steadily for the past two decades [1].

But the statistics, as shocking as they are, do not capture the human reality. They do not capture the teenager who feels so hopeless that she cannot get out of bed. They do not capture the middle-aged man who has lost his job and his sense of purpose and turned to alcohol to numb the pain. They do not capture the elderly person dying alone in their apartment, their body not discovered for weeks, a phenomenon so common in Japan that they have a word for it: *kodokushi*, lonely death.

Suicide remains a devastating outcome. In 2021, an estimated 727,000 people took their own lives. That is one death every 45 seconds. Suicide is now the leading cause of death among young people across all countries and socioeconomic contexts. And despite decades of public health initiatives and increased awareness, progress in reducing suicide rates is glacially slow. On the current trajectory, the world will achieve only a 12 percent reduction in suicide deaths by 2030, far short of the one-third reduction called for by the United Nations Sustainable Development Goals [1].

What is particularly striking is that this mental health crisis is not confined to the poor or the marginalised. It is epidemic among the wealthy, the educated, the privileged. In wealthy Western nations, we have more material abundance than any generation in history. We have more freedom, more technology, more access to information and entertainment. And yet we are more depressed, more anxious, more suicidal than ever before.

Why? The answer lies in what we explored in Chapter 11: the meaning crisis. When a society abandons the moral frameworks that give life meaning and purpose, people are left adrift. They are told that they are free to define their own values, to create their own meaning. But the result, for many, is not liberation but paralysis. Without a framework, without a sense of obligation to something larger than themselves, without a clear sense of right and wrong, people struggle to find reasons to keep going.

The opioid crisis that has devastated communities across North America is a symptom of this deeper malaise. Yes, there were pharmaceutical companies that aggressively marketed painkillers. Yes, there was a failure of regulation and oversight. But the reason so many people became addicted, the reason they continued using even as their lives fell apart, was not just the addictive power of the drug. It was the absence of meaning. In communities where factories had closed, where jobs had disappeared, where the traditional sources of meaning—work, family, community—had evaporated, the opioid offered an escape. It was not just an escape from physical pain, but from existential pain, from the unbearable emptiness of a life without purpose.

Similarly, the rising rates of suicide among middle-aged men in wealthy countries cannot be explained by poverty or lack of access to material goods. These men have money. They have homes. They have the material trappings of success. But they have lost the sense of purpose that gave their lives meaning. They were told that their role was to be breadwinners, to provide for their families. But in a world where that role is no longer valued, where they are told that their contribution is not needed, they are left adrift. Without a sense of purpose, without a sense that their lives matter, suicide becomes a rational response to an irrational situation.

The Political Fragmentation

In 2022, the Pew Research Center conducted a survey of American political attitudes. They found that 72 percent of Republicans and 63 percent of Democrats viewed the opposing party not just as wrong, but as a threat to the nation's well-being. This is not a disagreement about policy. This is not a difference of opinion about how to best serve the common good. This is a fundamental breakdown in the ability to see those who disagree with you as fellow citizens, as people with legitimate concerns and perspectives, as human beings worthy of respect and consideration [2].

This is what happens when a society violates the commandments against coveting and against bearing false witness on a massive scale. When people are constantly told that their political opponents are not just wrong but evil, that they are motivated by malice rather than genuine conviction, that they represent an existential threat, the possibility of democratic discourse disappears. You cannot reason with someone you believe to be evil. You cannot compromise with someone you believe to be a threat. You can only fight.

And so democracies begin to fail. Not because of external invasion or military coup, but because the citizens lose the ability to cooperate with one another. They retreat into tribal enclaves, each convinced of their own righteousness and the depravity of their opponents. They consume media that confirms their biases and amplifies their outrage. They interpret ambiguous events in the worst possible light. They assume bad faith. They assume conspiracy.

The result is a kind of cold civil war. Not yet hot enough to involve violence on a large scale, but hot enough to make normal democratic functioning impossible. Legislation becomes impossible because there is no possibility of compromise. Institutions become paralysed because they are staffed by people who no longer trust one another. The government becomes unable to respond to crises because the response itself becomes a political battleground.

This is not unique to the United States. We see it in the United Kingdom, where Brexit has fractured the nation. We see it in France, where political polarisation has reached levels not seen since the Fourth Republic. We see it in Australia, where climate change has become so politicised that rational discussion is nearly impossible. We see it everywhere in the Western world: the breakdown of the shared moral framework that allows a diverse society to function.

The Cascade of Failure

What is remarkable about these failures—the institutional collapse, the mental health epidemic, the political fragmentation—is that they are not independent phenomena. They are interconnected. They feed on one another. They create a cascade of failure that accelerates as it goes.

The loss of trust in institutions leads to political polarisation. Political polarisation leads to the breakdown of democratic discourse. The breakdown of democratic discourse leads to the failure of institutions to address collective problems. The failure of institutions leads to further loss of trust. And round and round it goes, each failure reinforcing the others, each breakdown making recovery more difficult.

Meanwhile, the meaning crisis deepens. As institutions fail, as political conflict intensifies, as the social fabric tears, people become increasingly desperate for some source of meaning, some sense that their lives matter. In the absence of a coherent moral framework, they turn to whatever is available: conspiracy theories, radical ideologies, addictive substances, compulsive consumption. These offer a temporary sense of meaning, a temporary sense of belonging, but they do not address the underlying problem. And so the crisis deepens.

The mental health epidemic is both a cause and a consequence of this cascade. As people become more depressed and anxious, they become less able to engage in the kind of rational, generous discourse that democracy requires. They become more reactive, more tribal, more susceptible to manipulation. And as the political and institutional environment becomes more hostile, more chaotic, more unpredictable, people become more depressed and anxious.

It is a vicious cycle. And there is no easy way out. You cannot restore trust by fiat. You cannot restore meaning by government decree. You cannot restore the ability to cooperate simply by deciding to cooperate. These things are built slowly, through thousands of small acts of integrity, through the gradual accumulation of evidence that people can be trusted, that institutions are acting in good faith, that there is a shared reality and a shared set of values that we can all agree on.

The Final Argument: You Can Reject the Source, But You Cannot Escape the System

And so we arrive at the final, and perhaps most important, insight. Throughout this book, we have been exploring the Ten Commandments as a description of reality. We have argued that they work not because they are imposed by divine authority, but because they are aligned with the deep structure of human psychology, human biology, and human society. We have argued that they are a compression algorithm for the solutions to fundamental cooperation problems.

But there is a corollary to this argument, and it is this: you cannot escape the structure by rejecting the source. You can decide that you don't believe in God. You can decide that the commandments are outdated relics of a primitive worldview. You can decide that you are going to build a society on different principles, on the basis of pure reason, or pure freedom, or pure self-interest. But you cannot escape the consequences of violating the structure.

This is the ultimate lesson of the past several decades. We have tried to build a society without the commandments. We have tried to liberate ourselves from the constraints of traditional morality. And what we have discovered is that the constraints were not arbitrary. They were not oppressive. They were the load-bearing walls of the structure. Remove them, and the building collapses.

You can reject God. But you cannot reject the fact that humans need meaning, and that meaning is most reliably found in commitment to something larger than yourself. You can reject the prohibition against adultery. But you cannot reject the fact that betrayal destroys the attachment bonds that are the foundation of family and society. You can reject the commandment against bearing false witness. But you cannot reject the fact that trust is the operating system of society, and that lies corrode it.

The laws work because they describe reality. And reality does not care whether you believe in it or not. You can jump off a cliff and deny the law of gravity, but you will still fall. You can violate the commandments and deny their validity, but you will still experience the consequences. The structure is written into the fabric of the universe. It is written into our brains, our bodies, our relationships, our societies. And no amount of ideological conviction can change that.

This is not an argument for dogmatism. This is not an argument for blind obedience to religious authority. This is an argument for humility. It is an argument for recognising that the moral frameworks that have emerged across human history are not accidents. They are solutions to real problems. They are the accumulated wisdom of countless generations of human beings trying to figure out how to live together, how to flourish, how to build societies that work.

And if we are going to rebuild our societies, if we are going to address the cascading failures we are experiencing, we are going to have to start by recognising this. We are going to have to acknowledge that the commandments are not constraints on freedom, but the conditions for freedom. We are going to have to recognise that the moral frameworks we have rejected are not obstacles to progress, but the foundations on which progress is built.

EPILOGUE: The Return of Ancient Wisdom

In the spring of 2023, a remarkable thing happened in the publishing world. A book appeared on bestseller lists across the Western world. It was not a self-help book, though it contained practical advice. It was not a religious text, though it drew heavily on religious traditions. It was a book about meaning, about how to live a life of purpose and significance in a secular age. The book was *The Courage to Be Disliked*, a dialogue between a philosopher and a young man exploring the ideas of Alfred Adler, a contemporary of Freud who argued that the primary human motivation is not pleasure or power, but the search for meaning and contribution.

The book became a phenomenon. Millions of copies were sold. It was translated into dozens of languages. Young people, in particular, flocked to it. And the reason was simple: they were hungry. Hungry for meaning. Hungry for a framework that could help them make sense of their lives. Hungry for something to believe in.

This hunger is not unique to Japan, where the book originated. It is visible everywhere in the Western world. There is a resurgence of interest in ancient philosophical traditions—Stoicism, Buddhism, Taoism. There is a revival of interest in ritual and community, even among the secular. There is a growing recognition that the purely materialist worldview, the idea that the purpose of life is to accumulate wealth and consume goods, has failed to deliver on its promise of happiness.

Young people are turning to meditation, to yoga, to practices that their grandparents would have recognised as spiritual disciplines. They are seeking out communities, both online and offline, where they can find connection and meaning. They are asking questions about purpose and significance that their parents' generation was told were naive or outdated. They are, in effect, rediscovering the wisdom that their societies had rejected.

This is not a return to dogmatism. It is not a wholesale rejection of modernity or science. It is something more subtle and more interesting. It is a recognition that the Enlightenment project, for all its achievements, was incomplete. That reason alone is not sufficient to answer the deepest questions about how to live. That meaning cannot be manufactured or purchased. That it must be discovered, and that the discoveries of previous generations can guide us in that search.

Why These Ideas Are Re-Emerging

The re-emergence of ancient wisdom is not accidental. It is a response to the failure of the alternatives. For the past century, Western intellectuals have been engaged in a grand project of deconstruction. They have subjected every traditional belief, every conventional morality, every inherited framework to ruthless criticism. And in many cases, this criticism was justified. Traditional morality did contain elements of oppression, of injustice, of irrationality. The project of liberation was, in many respects, necessary and good.

But the deconstruction went too far. In our eagerness to tear down the old structures, we failed to build anything to replace them. We created a vacuum. And nature, as they say, abhors a vacuum. Into that vacuum have rushed all manner of substitutes: consumer culture, political ideology, social media, addiction. None of them satisfy. None of them provide the meaning that humans desperately need.

And so people are returning to the old frameworks, not because they have been convinced by religious authority, but because they have discovered, through painful experience, that the alternatives don't work. They have tried the purely secular approach. They have tried to build their lives on the basis of individual autonomy and self-interest. And they have found that it leaves them empty.

This is not a religious revival, at least not in the traditional sense. Most of the people who are rediscovering ancient wisdom are not becoming orthodox believers. They are not joining churches or mosques or temples. They are doing something more interesting: they are extracting the wisdom from these traditions while leaving behind the dogmatism. They are asking: what is true about these teachings? What insights do they contain? How can we apply them in a modern context?

The Hunger for Meaning in a Secular Age

The irony is that the hunger for meaning is strongest among those who have rejected religious belief. Secular people, by and large, do not believe in God. They do not believe that there is an objective moral order written into the fabric of the universe. And yet they desperately want to believe that their lives matter, that their choices have significance, that there is something worth living for beyond the satisfaction of their own desires.

This is not a contradiction. It is a recognition of a fundamental truth about human nature: we are meaning-making creatures. We cannot live without meaning. We will find it somewhere. If we do not find it in a coherent moral framework, we will find it in tribalism, in ideology, in addiction, in the endless pursuit of status and consumption. But we will find it somewhere.

The great gift of the religious traditions is that they have spent thousands of years exploring the question of meaning. They have developed sophisticated frameworks for understanding what makes a life worth living. They have identified the sources of meaning: connection to something transcendent, contribution to a community, the pursuit of virtue, the cultivation of wisdom. They have developed practices—prayer, meditation, ritual, community—that help people access these sources of meaning.

And the remarkable thing is that many of these insights do not depend on belief in God. You do not have to believe that the universe was created by a divine being to recognise that humans flourish when they are part of a community, when they are contributing to something larger than themselves, when they are pursuing virtue and wisdom. You do not have to believe in divine judgment to recognise that integrity and honesty are essential to a flourishing life. You do not have to believe in an afterlife to recognise that how you treat others matters, that your choices have consequences, that you have obligations to the people around you.

This is the great discovery of the secular age: that the wisdom of the religious traditions can be extracted and applied without the religious framework. That you can live according to the commandments without believing that they came from God. That you can build a meaningful life on the basis of reason and evidence and experience, rather than on the basis of faith and authority.

The Possibility of Renewal Without Dogma

And so we arrive at the final possibility, the one that gives hope for the future. It is possible to renew our moral frameworks without returning to dogmatism. It is possible to rebuild our institutions on the basis of the ancient wisdom, while remaining fully modern, fully rational, fully scientific.

This would require a fundamental shift in how we think about morality. Instead of seeing it as a set of arbitrary rules imposed by authority, we would see it as a description of reality, as a map of the territory of human flourishing. Instead of asking "Is this rule true?" we would ask "Does this rule work? Does it lead to flourishing? Is it aligned with human nature and human psychology?"

And the remarkable thing is that when we ask these questions, we find that the ancient wisdom is, by and large, correct. The commandments work. They work because they are aligned with how humans are actually built. They work because they describe the conditions under which human beings flourish. They work because they are the accumulated wisdom of countless generations of human beings trying to figure out how to live together.

This does not mean that we should return uncritically to traditional morality. There are elements of traditional morality that are oppressive, that are based on outdated understandings of human nature, that need to be reformed or abandoned. But it does mean that we should approach the task of moral renewal with humility. We should recognise that the frameworks we are rejecting are not simply obstacles to progress, but repositories of hard-won wisdom. We should ask ourselves: what is true about this? What can we learn from it? How can we apply it in a modern context?

This is the great work of our time. Not the deconstruction of the old frameworks—that work is largely complete, and much of it was necessary. But the reconstruction of moral frameworks that are grounded in evidence, in reason, in human experience, but that also draw on the wisdom of the past. Frameworks that can guide us toward flourishing, that can help us build societies that work, that can give our lives meaning and purpose.

The commandments are not a relic of the past. They are a blueprint for the future. Not only because they came from God, but also because they describe, with breathtaking accuracy, the conditions under which human beings flourish. And in a world that has lost its way, that is perhaps the most radical and revolutionary thing we could possibly discover.

The ancient wisdom is returning. Not as dogma, but as evidence. Not as authority, but as insight. Not as constraint, but as liberation. And in that return lies the possibility of renewal, of healing, of a future in which we can build societies that work, in which we can live lives of meaning and purpose, in which we can flourish.

The Path Forward

What would this renewal look like in practice? It would mean, first and foremost, a commitment to truth. Not truth as a relative construct, not truth as whatever serves our interests, but truth as an objective reality that we can discover and that we have an obligation to respect. It would mean rebuilding institutions on the foundation of integrity and honesty. It would mean holding ourselves and our leaders accountable when they lie.

It would mean recognising that the family is not an oppressive relic but the fundamental unit of human flourishing. It would mean rebuilding the culture of commitment, of fidelity, of the willingness to sacrifice for those we love. It would mean creating space for genuine community, for face-to-face connection, for the kind of embodied presence that our brains are wired for.

It would mean rebuilding the culture of work and contribution, recognising that human beings need to feel that they are part of something, that their efforts matter, that they are contributing to the common good. It would mean creating economic systems that reward integrity and punish deception, that allow people to build meaningful lives, that do not reduce human beings to mere consumers.

It would mean recognising that rest and renewal are not luxuries but necessities. It would mean creating space in our lives for contemplation, for connection with something transcendent, for the cultivation of wisdom and virtue.

And it would mean doing all of this not because we are commanded to by religious authority, but because we have discovered, through reason and evidence and experience, that this is how human beings flourish. This is how societies work. This is how we build a future worth living in.

The commandments are not a cage. They are a map. And in following that map, we do not diminish our freedom. We discover what freedom actually means: not the absence of all constraints, but the presence of the right constraints, the ones that align us with reality, with our own nature, and with one another.

A Final Word

This book has been an exploration of an ancient text through the lens of modern science, modern psychology, modern sociology. We have asked: why do these laws endure? Why do they appear across cultures and centuries? What is it about them that makes them so powerful, so resilient, so true?

And the answer, we have discovered, is not mystical or mysterious. It is grounded in the deepest truths about human nature. The commandments work because they describe reality. They work because they are aligned with how we are built. They work because they are the solutions that humanity has discovered, again and again, to the fundamental problems of living together.

We could reject the source. We could say that we do not believe in God, that we do not accept religious authority, that we are going to build our societies on different principles. But we cannot escape the sacred operating system. The structure is written into our brains, our bodies, our relationships, our societies. It is written into the fabric of reality itself.

And so the question that faces us now is not whether the commandments are true. They are. The question is whether we have the wisdom to recognise this, and the courage to rebuild our societies on their foundation. One option is to attempt to extract the wisdom from the religious traditions without the dogmatism - to see whether we can build a future that is both modern and moral, both rational and meaningful, both free and grounded in truth. Alternatively, you could read the Bible and believe it.

Either way, the ancient wisdom must prevail. If we want to rediscover ourselves. If we want to rediscover what it means to be human, what we need to flourish, what kind of societies allow us to thrive. And in that rediscovery lies hope. Hope that we can heal the divisions that tear us apart. Hope that we can rebuild the trust that holds us together. Hope that we can create a future in which all of us can flourish.

The commandments are calling us home. Not only to the past, but also to the future. Not to dogma, but to truth. Not to constraint, but to freedom. And in answering that call, we may yet discover that the ancient wisdom was not ancient at all. It was always new. It was always true. It was always waiting for us to find our way back.

References

A

Ainsworth, M. D. S., Blehar, M. C., Waters, E., & Wall, S. (1978). *Patterns of attachment: A psychological study of the strange situation*. Lawrence Erlbaum Associates.

Arendt, H. (1963). *Eichmann in Jerusalem: A report on the banality of evil*. Viking Press.

Austin, J. L. (1962). *How to do things with words*. Oxford University Press.

B

Bandura, A. (2016). *Moral disengagement: How people do harm and live with themselves*. Worth Publishers.

Bedrov, A., & Gable, S. L. (2023). How much is it weighing on you? Development and validation of the Secrecy Burden Scale. *Personality and Social Psychology Bulletin*, *50*(9), 1332–1347. https://doi.org/10.1177/01461672231172387

Berridge, K. C. (2009). 'Liking' and 'wanting' food rewards: Brain substrates and roles in eating disorders. *Physiology & Behavior*, *97*(5), 537–550. https://doi.org/10.1016/j.physbeh.2009.02.044

Berridge, K. C. (2009). Wanting and liking: Observations from the neuroscience and psychology laboratory. *Inquiry*, *52*(4), 378–398. https://doi.org/10.1080/00201740903087359

Besedovsky, L., Lange, T., & Born, J. (2012). Sleep and immune function. *Pflügers Archiv - European Journal of Physiology*, *463*(1), 121–137. https://doi.org/10.1007/s00424-011-1044-0

Blandón-Gitlin, I., Fenn, E., Masip, J., & Yoo, A. H. (2014). Cognitive-load approaches to detect deception: Searching for cognitive mechanisms. *Trends in Cognitive Sciences*, *18*(9), 441–444. https://doi.org/10.1016/j.tics.2014.05.004

Blumenthal, S. A., & Young, L. J. (2023). The neurobiology of love and pair bonding from human and animal perspectives. *Biology*, *12*(6), 844. https://doi.org/10.3390/biology12060844

Bowlby, J. (1969). *Attachment and loss: Vol. 1. Attachment*. Basic Books.

Brickman, P., Coates, D., & Janoff-Bulman, R. (1978). Lottery winners and accident victims: Is happiness relative? *Journal of Personality and Social Psychology*, *36*(8), 917–927. https://doi.org/10.1037/0022-3514.36.8.917

Bromberg-Martin, E. S., Matsumoto, M., & Hikosaka, O. (2010). Dopamine in motivational control: Rewarding, aversive, and alerting. *Neuron*, *68*(5), 815–834. https://doi.org/10.1016/j.neuron.2010.11.022

Bushkin, H., van Niekerk, R., & Stroud, L. (2021). Searching for meaning in chaos: Viktor Frankl's story. *European Journal of Psychology*, *17*(3), 233–242. https://doi.org/10.5964/ejop.5439

C

CarBuzz. (2024, October 12). *Fact or fiction: Have people driven into lakes because of navigation?* https://carbuzz.com/fact-or-fiction-have-people-driven-into-lakes-because-of-navigation/

Carreyrou, J. (2018). *Bad blood: Secrets and lies in a Silicon Valley startup*. Alfred A. Knopf.

D

De Soto, H. (2000). *The mystery of capital: Why capitalism triumphs in the West and fails everywhere else*. Basic Books.

Diener, E., Lucas, R. E., & Scollon, C. N. (2006). Beyond the hedonic treadmill: Revising the adaptation theory of well-being. *American Psychologist, 61*(4), 305–314. https://doi.org/10.1037/0003-066X.61.4.305

E

Emmons, R. A., & McCullough, M. E. (2003). Counting blessings versus burdens: An experimental investigation of gratitude and subjective well-being in daily life. *Journal of Personality and Social Psychology, 84*(2), 377–389. https://doi.org/10.1037/0022-3514.84.2.377

Engen, H. G., & Singer, T. (2013). Empathy circuits. *Current Opinion in Neurobiology, 23*(2), 275–282. https://doi.org/10.1016/j.conb.2012.11.003

F

Festinger, L. (1954). A theory of social comparison processes. *Human Relations, 7*(2), 117–140. https://doi.org/10.1177/001872675400700202

Fiske, S. T., Cuddy, A. J. C., Glick, P., & Xu, J. (2002). A model of (often mixed) stereotype content: Competence and warmth respectively follow from perceived status and competition. *Journal of Personality and Social Psychology, 82*(6), 878–902. https://doi.org/10.1037/0022-3514.82.6.878

Frank, A. (2021, December 9). What is scientism, and why is it a mistake? *Big Think*. https://bigthink.com/13-8/science-vs-scientism/

Frankl, V. E. (2006). *Man's search for meaning*. Beacon Press. (Original work published 1946)

G

George, C., Kaplan, N., & Main, M. (1985). *Adult Attachment Interview* [Unpublished manuscript]. University of California, Berkeley.

Grubbs, J. B., James, A. S., Warmke, B., & Tosi, J. (2022). Moral grandstanding, narcissism, and self-reported responses to the COVID-19 crisis. *Journal of Research in Personality, 97*, 104187. https://doi.org/10.1016/j.jrp.2021.104187

H

Harris, L. T., & Fiske, S. T. (2011). Dehumanized perception: A psychological means to facilitate atrocities, torture, and genocide? *Zeitschrift für Psychologie/Journal of Psychology, 219*(3), 175–181. https://doi.org/10.1027/2151-2604/a000065

I

Iacoboni, M. (2008). *Mirroring people: The new science of how we connect with others*. Farrar, Straus and Giroux.

J

Jost, J. T., Baldassarri, D. S., & Druckman, J. N. (2022). Cognitive–motivational mechanisms of political polarization in social-communicative contexts. *Nature Reviews Psychology, 1*(10), 560–576. https://doi.org/10.1038/s44159-022-00093-5

K

Kahneman, D., Knetsch, J. L., & Thaler, R. H. (1991). Anomalies: The endowment effect, loss aversion, and status quo bias. *Journal of Economic Perspectives, 5*(1), 193–206. https://doi.org/10.1257/jep.5.1.193

Korzybski, A. (1933). *Science and sanity: An introduction to non-Aristotelian systems and general semantics*. International Non-Aristotelian Library Publishing Company.

Kruglanski, A. W., & Webster, D. M. (1996). Motivated closing of the mind: "Seizing" and "freezing." *Psychological Review, 103*(2), 263–283. https://doi.org/10.1037/0033-295X.103.2.263

L

Lacy, J. W., & Stark, C. E. L. (2013). The neuroscience of memory: Implications for the courtroom. *Nature Reviews Neuroscience, 14*(9), 649–658. https://doi.org/10.1038/nrn3563

Lee, J. K. (2020). The effects of social comparison orientation on psychological well-being in social networking sites: Serial mediation of perceived social support and self-esteem. *Current Psychology, 41*(9), 6247–6259. https://doi.org/10.1007/s12144-020-01114-3

Liana, W. (2020, March 11). All the lonely people: The atomized generation. *Erraticus*. http://erraticus.co/2020/03/11/atomized-generation-community-atomization-loneliness/

Loftus, E. F. (1975). Leading questions and the eyewitness report. *Cognitive Psychology, 7*(4), 560–572. https://doi.org/10.1016/0010-0285(75)90023-7

Lynch, R. (2020, November 22). Kin, tribes, and the dark side of identity. *Quillette*. https://quillette.com/2020/11/22/kin-tribes-and-the-dark-side-of-identity/

M

Main, M., & Hesse, E. (1990). Parents' unresolved traumatic experiences are related to infant disorganized attachment status: Is frightened and/or frightening parental behavior the linking mechanism? In M. T. Greenberg, D. Cicchetti, & E. M. Cummings (Eds.), *Attachment in the preschool years: Theory, research, and intervention* (pp. 161–182). University of Chicago Press.

Main, M., & Solomon, J. (1990). Procedures for identifying infants as disorganized/disoriented during the Ainsworth Strange Situation. In M. T. Greenberg, D. Cicchetti, & E. M. Cummings (Eds.), *Attachment in the preschool years: Theory, research, and intervention* (pp. 121–160). University of Chicago Press.

Menon, V. (2023). 20 years of the default mode network: A review and synthesis. *Neuron, 111*(16), 2469–2487. https://doi.org/10.1016/j.neuron.2023.04.023

N

Newport, C. (2016). *Deep work: Rules for focused success in a distracted world.* Grand Central Publishing.

Nyseth Brehm, H. (2017). Subnational determinants of killing in Rwanda. *Criminology, 55*(1), 5–31. https://doi.org/10.1111/1745-9125.12131

P

Pang, A. S. K. (2016). *Rest: Why you get more done when you work less.* Basic Books.

Pariser, E. (2011). *The filter bubble: What the Internet is hiding from you.* Penguin Press.

Poydock, M., & Zhang, J. (2024). *More than $1.5 billion in stolen wages recovered for workers between 2021 and 2023.*

Economic Policy Institute. https://www.epi.org/publication/stolen-wages-2021-2023/

R

Raichle, M. E. (2015). The brain's default mode network. *Annual Review of Neuroscience, 38*, 433–447. https://doi.org/10.1146/annurev-neuro-071013-014030

Raichle, M. E., MacLeod, A. M., Snyder, A. Z., Powers, W. J., Gusnard, D. A., & Shulman, G. L. (2001). A default mode of brain function. *Proceedings of the National Academy of Sciences, 98*(2), 676–682. https://doi.org/10.1073/pnas.98.2.676

Rizzolatti, G., & Sinigaglia, C. (2008). *Mirrors in the brain: How our minds share actions and emotions.* Oxford University Press.

Ronson, J. (2015). *So you've been publicly shamed.* Riverhead Books.

S

Saenger, L. Y. (2022). *Respect your elders? The economic origins and political consequences of attitudes toward the aged* [Undergraduate honors thesis]. Harvard University.

Sansone, R. A., & Sansone, L. A. (2014). "I'm your number one fan"—A clinical look at celebrity worship. *Innovations in Clinical Neuroscience, 11*(1–2), 39–43.

Schulte, B. (2014). *Overwhelmed: Work, love, and play when no one has the time.* Sarah Crichton Books.

Stallen, M., Rossi, F., Heijne, A., Smidts, A., De Dreu, C. K., & Sanfey, A. G. (2018). Neurobiological mechanisms of responding to injustice. *Journal of Neuroscience, 38*(12),

2944–2954. https://doi.org/10.1523/JNEUROSCI.1242-17.2018

Straus, S. (2016). *Fundamentals of genocide and mass atrocity prevention*. United States Holocaust Memorial Museum.

T

Tosi, J., & Warmke, B. (2020). *Grandstanding: The use and abuse of moral talk*. Oxford University Press.

Twenge, J. M., & Campbell, W. K. (2009). *The narcissism epidemic: Living in the age of entitlement*. Free Press.

V

van IJzendoorn, M. H. (1995). Adult attachment representations, parental responsiveness, and infant attachment: A meta-analysis on the predictive validity of the Adult Attachment Interview. *Psychological Bulletin, 117*(3), 387–403. https://doi.org/10.1037/0033-2909.117.3.387

Vasist, P. N., Chatterjee, D., & Krishnan, S. (2023). The polarizing impact of political disinformation and hate speech: A cross-country configural narrative. *Information Systems Frontiers, 26*(5), 1863–1895. https://doi.org/10.1007/s10796-023-10390-w

Vosoughi, S., Roy, D., & Aral, S. (2018). The spread of true and false news online. *Science, 359*(6380), 1146–1151. https://doi.org/10.1126/science.aap9559

W

Waite, L. J., & Gallagher, M. (2000). *The case for marriage: Why married people are happier, healthier, and better off financially*. Doubleday.

Wallace, D. F. (2009). *This is water: Some thoughts, delivered on a significant occasion, about living a compassionate life*. Little, Brown and Company. (Based on 2005 commencement address at Kenyon College)

Y

Young, L. J., & Wang, Z. (2004). The neurobiology of pair bonding. *Nature Neuroscience, 7*(10), 1048–1054. https://doi.org/10.1038/nn1327

Z

Zak, P. J. (2017, January–February). The neuroscience of trust. *Harvard Business Review*, 84–90. https://hbr.org/2017/01/the-neuroscience-of-trust

Zmigrod, L., Rentfrow, P. J., & Robbins, T. W. (2019). Cognitive inflexibility predicts extremist attitudes. *Frontiers in Psychology, 10*, 989. https://doi.org/10.3389/fpsyg.2019.00989

www.ingramcontent.com/pod-product-compliance
Lightning Source LLC
Chambersburg PA
CBHW071954100426
42738CB00043B/2901